QUANTUM FRONTIER: DEMYSTIFYING THE NEXT TECH REVOLUTION

PREFACE

I n a world where technological advancements often hit us like successive waves, quantum computing emerges not as a mere ripple but as a seismic shift—a revolution promising to redefine reality itself. As the author of "Quantum Frontier: Demystifying the Next Tech Revolution," my goal is to turn this promise into something tangible and comprehensible, bridging the esoteric with the everyday.

My journey into the quantum realm began not in a lecture hall, but in the lively environments where theory translates into application—research labs, tech innovation hubs, and industry think tanks. Here, quantum computing wasn't simply the subject of speculative thought; it was a nascent force, pulsating with possibilities and on the cusp of reshaping how we interact with the digital and physical worlds.

My motivation for writing this book stems from awe and a sense of duty: awe at the transformative power of quantum computing to redefine fields as diverse as cryptography, pharmacology, and artificial intelligence, and a duty to demystify and share this profound knowledge. I envision a future where understanding quantum computing is not a privilege, but a necessity for innovators, business leaders, students, and the curious observer.

Throughout this book, my intention is not only to inform but also to transform perspectives. Quantum computing is often cloaked in a veil of complexity; however, the chapters that follow endeavor to lift that veil, making the intricacies accessible and the immense potential clear. From the foundational principles in Chapter 1 to the visionary forecasts in Chapter 10, each page is crafted to equip you, the reader, with insights needed to navigate and contribute to this unfolding frontier.

I hope to inspire not just understanding, but action. As industries pivot towards this quantum era, the need for a skilled and prepared workforce becomes paramount. This book outlines a clearer path to foster curiosity and confidence, encouraging you to step forward as a participant in this tech revolution.

"Quantum Frontier" is more than a title; it is an invitation. An invitation to explore the intersections of quantum physics and practical innovation, to reconsider what you know about technology, and to engage with one of the most thrilling paradigms of our time.

In reading this book, you hold in your hands a potential catalyst for change—a chance to see beyond the current limits of technology and into a future where quantum principles redefine our very understanding of computation and problem-solving. As you turn the pages, may the journey expand your horizon, fuel your innovation, and deepen your appreciation for the mind-bending science that is quantum computing.

TABLE OF CONTENTS

INTRODUCTION: QUANTUM BEGINNINGS

I n an ordinary garage nestled within the bustling metropolis of San Francisco, amidst a cacophony of hammers, whirring machines, and the occasional hiss of soldering irons, I discovered a world alive with infinite possibilities. This space, cluttered with quirky contraptions and awash with the scent of smoldering metal, belonged to my grandfather—a tinkerer at heart, whose curiosity beguiled me during my formative years. It was here that I first glimpsed the boundless interplay of physics and digital technology, an introduction to the art of the possible, if you will. Today, as we stand on the precipice of yet another technological renaissance, spurred not by silicon and circuits alone but by the enigmatic whispers of quantum mechanics, I invite you to journey alongside me into the depths of this fascinating frontier.

The term "quantum" might echo with resounding complexity, inspiring awe and puzzlement in equal measure. Conceived in the early 20th century by pioneers like Max Planck and Albert Einstein, quantum mechanics began its life as a theoretical pursuit—a radical exploration of the universal fabric that defied classical intuition. Fast forward a century, and the esoteric equations that once resided exclusively within ivory towers now underpin the technological underpinnings of a forthcoming revolution. "Quantum Frontier: Demystifying the Next Tech Revolution" aspires to unravel this intricate tapestry, translating convoluted jargon into narratives as electrifying as they are enlightening.

Within the shimmering domain of quantum computing, science fiction melds seamlessly with science fact. At its core is the qubit, an enigmatic entity that straddles multiple states of existence. Unlike classical bits, constrained by binary limitations of ones and zeroes, qubits exploit the phenomena of superposition and entanglement, enabling them to traverse realms of parallel universes. The ramifications of this duality surpass the capabilities of contemporary computing paradigms, setting the stage for innovations hitherto deemed impossible.

This book seeks to illuminate the path of quantum discovery, presenting this avant-garde science not as an insurmountable mystery, but as an accessible paradigm poised to reshape our technological reality. From enhancing cryptographic measures that safeguard our digital secrets to expediting drug discovery in ways only dreamt of by pharmaceutical pioneers, quantum computing stands on the cusp of unleashing transformative change. Its influence radiates through industries as diverse as logistics and finance, promising optimizations previously beyond reach.

But let me assure you, dear reader, that this tome does more than merely catalogue existing advancements. It is a clarion call for participation, understanding, and ethical consideration. As the tentacles of quantum technology weave through the modern tapestry, issues of access and ethical deployment emerge as urgent topics demanding our collective scrutiny. What does it mean to democratize a technology as potent as quantum computing? How do we ensure its benefits are universally accessible and ethically sound?

Yet, the marvels of quantum computing are not without their challenges or misconceptions. The theoretical elegance of qubits often contrasts starkly with the practical hurdles of error rates and decoherence, the process by which quantum information becomes corrupted. It is upon these challenging vistas that our narrative casts a diagnostic eye, dispelling myths and unveiling the profound work still to be done.

Throughout "Quantum Frontier," I draw upon real-world scenarios, while occasionally employing fictional names to uphold the confidentiality of innovative minds who have shared their invaluable insights. Whether recounting the saga of a start-up perfecting quantum-resistant encryption or a pharmaceutical titan accelerating molecular simulations, the lessons and visions imparted serve as both guide and inspiration.

This introduction is but your first step into a broader exploration —a prelude to comprehending the symbiotic dance between technology and humankind, and the roles we are destined to play in shaping a quantum future. By embarking on this journey, equipped with curiosity and reflection, you participate in envisioning a world that balances digital mastery with humanistic values.

As with any profound undertaking, the essence of understanding is inextricably linked to its teaching and communication. I stand here not as an omniscient purveyor of quantum truths, but rather as a fellow seeker, navigating the intersection of science and imagination. The chapters that unfold beyond this point will delineate the nuances of quantum mechanics, the birth of quantum computing, and their industry applications, while never losing sight of the broader social implications.

Through this narrative, my hope is twofold: to inform and to inspire. May you emerge from this exploration ready to challenge assumptions, pursue innovations, and ultimately, contribute to the quantum dialogue that will shape our tomorrow. In doing so, you align with an illustrious cadre of thinkers, dreamers, and doers dedicated to forging the path forward in this kaleidoscopically advancing era.

This journey doesn't end at our final chapter, for as quantum principles reveal, solutions give rise to new questions in an ever-evolving enquiry—a perpetual, dynamic quest asking us to look beyond the visible, to question the fundamental, and to unearth the extraordinary. Together, we will traverse this multifaceted frontier, unlocking a gateway to endless potential and possibility.

So, I invite you, curious traveler, to step boldly into the quantum realm. The frontier awaits—teeming with untapped discoveries and stories yet to unfold.

CHAPTER 1: UNDERSTANDING QUANTUM MECHANICS – FROM EINSTEIN TO QUBITS

I n the annals of scientific revolution, few domains challenge our fundamental perception of reality as profoundly as quantum mechanics. As we embark on this journey, we enter a world where intuition falters and imagination prevails —a world where the established laws of classical physics are juxtaposed with the enigmatic principles of the subatomic realm. Chapter 1 of "Quantum Frontier: Demystifying the Next Tech Revolution" guides you through this intellectual odyssey, bridging the epochal insights of early quantum pioneers to the cutting-edge innovations that promise to redefine technology as we know it.

Our exploration begins at the dawn of the 20th century, an era marked by transformative discoveries that shattered the conventional wisdom of Newtonian physics. We delve into the revolutionary thoughts of Albert Einstein, Max Planck, and

Niels Bohr, whose groundbreaking theories collectively forged a new paradigm—one that dared to propose that light could behave as both particle and wave, and that energy levels were quantized rather than continuous. This historical narrative not only celebrates the audacity of scientific minds unafraid to defy tradition but also sets the stage for understanding how these early insights laid the foundation for modern quantum mechanics.

From there, we delve into the heart of quantum theory itself, exploring core principles that continue to baffle yet intrigue: superposition and entanglement. These concepts invite us to suspend disbelief, to imagine particles existing in multiple states at once and being inextricably linked, regardless of distance. Through accessible explanations and vivid examples, this chapter elucidates these principles, forming the theoretical underpinning crucial for grasping the audacious leap from theoretical physics to quantum computation.

Building upon these fundamental concepts, we transition to the birth of quantum computing—a revolutionary shift from theory to potential enterprise. What were once mere academic curiosities have now become the vanguards in the quest to surpass the limits of classical computing. Here, we introduce the provocative idea that quantum mechanics could be harnessed to exponentially enhance computational power, unlocking capabilities unimaginable within the confines of classical systems.

Central to this technological renaissance are qubits, the fundamental units of quantum information. This chapter deciphers the complexities of qubits, highlighting their ability to exist in multiple states simultaneously and thus perform complex calculations with remarkable efficiency. Analogies to classical computing serve to bridge the conceptual gap, demonstrating how these quantum units hold the key to technological transformations yet to come.

Finally, we synthesize these intricate threads by showcasing the nascent integration of quantum mechanics into practical computing applications. Through early experiments and ongoing advancements, we reveal how foundational scientific principles are materializing into tangible innovations, offering a preview of the vast potential awaiting on the horizon.

"Understanding Quantum Mechanics – From Einstein to Qubits" provides not just an academic overview, but an invitation to witness a grand narrative unfolding. This chapter heralds the advent of a new technological epoch, beckoning readers to explore the role of quantum mechanics as both a scientific marvel and an impetus for the next wave of technological advances. As we stand on the brink of this revolution, we discover that while quantum mechanics may defy intuition, it is undeniably guiding us towards a future brimming with possibilities.

The Dawn of Quantum Mechanics

In the annals of scientific history, few epochs are as transformative as the early 20th century, a period that witnessed the birth of quantum mechanics—a revolutionary leap that reframed our understanding of the universe. This era was marked by the intellectual daring of unparalleled minds such as Albert Einstein, Max Planck, and Niels Bohr, whose pioneering contributions laid the bedrock for what would become one of the most significant scientific paradigms of modern times.

The groundwork of quantum mechanics was unpredictably sown at the meeting point between classical physics and the limitations of the known scientific laws. Max Planck, in 1900, inadvertently set the stage with his introduction of the quantum of action, now universally known as Planck's constant. Tasked with solving the blackbody radiation problem, Planck proposed that energy could be emitted or absorbed in discrete packets, or "quanta," rather than continuously, as classical physics had previously assumed.

This radical idea began to illuminate the inadequacies of classical theories when applied to atomic and subatomic scales.

Planck's quanta concept ignited a chain reaction that would forever alter the landscape of physics. Enter Albert Einstein in 1905, whose seminal work on the photoelectric effect challenged classical electromagnetism and supported Planck's hypothesis. Einstein theorized that light itself could be quantized into "photons," discrete energy packets, an insight that not only reinforced the quantum narrative but also earned him the Nobel Prize in Physics in 1921. By suggesting that particles such as electrons could behave both like particles and waves, Einstein ventured into the labyrinthine dualities that would characterize quantum theory.

While Planck and Einstein laid foundational stones, it was Niels Bohr who constructed the first quantum model of the atom, further challenging Newtonian physics. Bohr's model introduced the idea of quantized electron orbits, arguing that electrons exist in stable orbits without radiating energy but jump between these orbits when they absorb or emit quanta of energy. This model provided explanations for the spectral lines of hydrogen —an experimental puzzle that had long baffled scientists— and cemented the quantum framework's capacity to articulate observed phenomena that eluded classical interpretation.

Together, these pioneers dared to traverse the hazy boundaries of the unknown and embarked upon an intellectual voyage that probed the very fabric of reality. The implications of their ideas transcended pure science, venturing into the realms of technology, philosophy, and society. While initially metaphysical musings, their discoveries laid the groundwork for technologies that, a century later, are beginning to reshape our world.

A compelling real-life analogy can help convey the radical nature of these early quantum breakthroughs. Imagine you are in a world where everyone uses rotary phones—reliable and predictable tools of communication. Then, suddenly, a new device arrives, a smartphone with touch interaction, internet access, and apps. To the uninitiated, it seems almost magical, its capabilities far surpassing the linear expectations of its forebears. Similarly, quantum mechanics introduced concepts that were wildly non-intuitive compared to classical physics, yet their accuracy in explaining and predicting phenomena was undeniable.

As we pivot to explore the core principles of this nascent field, understanding these historical milestones empowers us to appreciate the scientific bravado required to accept, and eventually embrace, the counterintuitive truths of quantum mechanics. Moving forward, we will delve into the intriguing concepts of superposition and entanglement, the cornerstones that defy classical logic and hold the keys to our quantum future.

The Core Principles – Superposition and Entanglement

In the mysterious realm of quantum mechanics, two concepts stand at the forefront: superposition and entanglement. These ideas form the bedrock upon which much of quantum theory is built, challenging our classical understandings of reality and opening new avenues for technological innovation.

Superposition is a principle that defies conventional wisdom by allowing particles to exist in multiple states at the same time. To appreciate this phenomenon, let's consider the famous thought experiment known as Schrödinger's cat. In this scenario, a cat is placed in a sealed box with a radioactive atom, a Geiger counter, and a poisonous vial. According to quantum theory, until the box is opened and the system is observed, the cat is simultaneously alive and dead. While this may seem perplexing, it effectively illustrates how quantum particles inhabit multiple potential states, collapsing into a singular reality only upon observation. In the framework of quantum computing, this allows qubits to perform numerous calculations simultaneously, vastly increasing computational power.

Entanglement, another cornerstone of quantum theory, describes a unique connection between particles, where the state of one instantly influences the state of the other, regardless of the distance between them. This "spooky action at a distance," as Einstein famously put it, defies the classic notion of locality. To grasp the practical implications, imagine two entangled particles: if you measure one particle's spin and find it to be clockwise, the other particle will have an anticlockwise spin —instantaneously, even if it resides on the other side of the universe. This phenomenon is not only fascinating but crucial for the advancement of quantum technologies, such as quantum cryptography, which promises unbreakable security through entangled particles.

To ground these abstract concepts in reality, let's explore how superposition and entanglement manifest in real-world applications. Consider the nascent field of quantum cryptography. Unlike classical encryption, which relies on mathematical algorithms that can potentially be broken given enough time and computational power, quantum cryptography leverages the principles of superposition and entanglement to ensure confidentiality. Through a method known as quantum key distribution (QKD), two parties can share encryption keys with absolute security. If an eavesdropper attempts to intercept the key, the act of measuring the quantum states will disturb them, alerting the legitimate parties to the breach.

In quantum computing, IBM's quantum computer, Qiskit, epitomizes how superposition and entanglement can be harnessed. The system uses these principles to solve complex optimization problems much faster than classical computers. For example, it's being deployed in the financial sector to simulate market behaviors, offering unprecedented insights for risk management and portfolio optimization.

As we unravel these foundational concepts, they lead us naturally into the next exploration of how these theories transition into the practical realm of quantum computing. By leveraging the peculiarities of superposition and entanglement, quantum computing is transforming from theoretical curiosity to a dynamic field reshaping our technological landscape.

The Transition to Quantum Computing

The dawn of the 20th century heralded not only a shift in scientific paradigms but also a reevaluation of how we process information. In the world of classical computing, dictated by the binary constraints of zeros and ones, the challenges of scalability and speed were becoming increasingly evident as we reached the physical and practical limitations of Moore's Law. It became clear that to breach these bottlenecks, a revolutionary approach was required—one that quantum mechanics seemed serendipitously positioned to offer.

At the heart of this burgeoning field of quantum computing lies the quest to exploit the unique phenomena of superposition and entanglement, which classical computing cannot address. Visionaries like Richard Feynman and David Deutsch proposed that by harnessing these principles, we could transcend conventional computing power, thus opening new realms of possibility.

To understand this evolution, consider the landscape of cryptography, a field heavily reliant on computational prowess. Classical encryption methods, based on complex mathematical problems, promised security against traditional computation. However, the prospect of quantum computing presents a game-changing dichotomy: simultaneously rendering current cryptographic techniques vulnerable and unlocking innovative means of secure communication through quantum encrypting methodologies like quantum key distribution.

For instance, Shor's algorithm, proposed by mathematician Peter Shor, eloquently illustrates this potential. It promises to factor large integers exponentially faster than the best-known classical algorithms, thereby undermining the security of popular encryption systems such as RSA. On the contrary, this potential vulnerability has also spurred innovations in post-quantum cryptography, fostering the development of secure alternatives against the threat of quantum decryption.

Furthermore, the transition into quantum computing is not merely theoretical. In the past decade, research institutions and technology companies like Google, IBM, and Rigetti Computing have pioneered the race towards building functional quantum computers. Consider Google's 2019 announcement of achieving "quantum supremacy"—a milestone where a quantum computer accomplished a task beyond the reach of the most powerful classical supercomputers. This achievement, though met with some skepticism, serves as a building block, proving quantum computations' realistic potential and pushing the boundaries of what's achievable.

Moreover, practical implementations are gradually emerging in fields beyond cryptography. In material science, quantum simulations could revolutionize our understanding of molecular and atomic interactions, enabling the discovery of new materials and drugs. Similarly, in logistics and finance, optimization problems, which are computationally intensive and resource-heavy, could become more feasible as quantum capabilities mature.

The transition to quantum computing signals not just an evolution in technology but a fundamental reimagining of how we harness the laws of nature for practical applications. This reimagining propels us toward the next subchapter, where we delve deeper into the basic units that form the backbone of quantum computing: qubits, and their vast potential to redefine computation as we know it. Let us now explore how qubits, the quantum equivalents of classical bits, are transforming these theoretical advancements into tangible computational frameworks.

Qubits – The Building Blocks

As we delve deeper into the mysterious world of quantum mechanics, we encounter the qubits—elemental units of quantum information that promise to redefine the very fabric of computation. While classical bits are confined to values of 0 or 1, qubits defy this binary restriction. A qubit can embody a superposition, coexisting in states of 0 and 1, an attribute that unlocks transformative potential for computational processes.

To fully grasp the concept of qubits, envision a classical bit as a coin resting flat on a table, unmistakably showing heads or tails. In contrast, a qubit is akin to a spinning coin, capable of representing both heads and tails at once. This ability to inherit dual states exponentially enhances the computing power, where a system with n qubits can simultaneously occupy 2^n states. Such an exponential leap empowers quantum computers to perform operations at a speed and scale unfathomable to classical systems.

Central to the functionality of qubits is the principle of entanglement. When qubits become entangled, the state of one qubit instantaneously influences the state of another, irrespective of the distance separating them. This phenomenon, often likened to an intricate cosmic dance, allows quantum computers to conduct parallel computations with extraordinary efficiency.

While the technical intricacies of qubits might seem arcane, practical examples illuminate their immense potential. Picture solving a labyrinthine puzzle where the correct path branches from myriad possibilities. Classical computers would need to sequentially explore each path, a laborious endeavor. In stark contrast, a quantum computer can evaluate all potential routes simultaneously. This aptitude is monumental in fields requiring substantial computational heft, such as cryptography or simulating chemical reactions for drug discoveries.

Consider, for instance, a real-world case study from the field of materials science. Scientists endeavoring to develop sustainable energy solutions utilize computational models to predict the performance of novel materials. In classical computing, simulating the interactions of particles within a potential solar cell material is computationally prohibitive due to the multiplicity of possible configurations. However, by leveraging qubits and their ability to manage vast combinatorial variabilities, researchers can simulate these interactions with unprecedented accuracy and speed, accelerating the journey toward more efficient solar cells.

Another illustrative scenario is the optimization of complex logistical networks. Companies managing global supply chains can deploy quantum algorithms to increase efficiency. Picture a vast network of routes and delivery times, where classical computing laboriously calculates optimal paths. Quantum computing, through qubit manipulation, assesses numerous pathways concurrently, offering optimal solutions that save time and reduce costs.

While harnessing the full potential of qubits remains on the frontier of scientific exploration, these examples underscore the paradigm-shifting opportunities they present. As we continue our exploration into quantum mechanics' practical applications, we will next examine how the foundational principles we've discussed converge to form the bedrock of quantum computing. This confluence fosters a new era where the boundaries of what we can compute are limited only by our imagination.

Bridging Quantum Mechanics

and Computing

As we stand at the threshold of a new era defined by quantum mechanics and computing, the synthesis of these fields heralds a transformation as profound as the initial shift from classical to quantum physics. This subchapter focuses on bridging theoretical quantum principles with practical computing innovations, offering a glimpse into how traditional understanding is being redefined to accommodate the quantum revolution.

Historically, the mathematics underpinning quantum mechanics —characterized by probabilities and wave functions—seemed abstract and inaccessible. Yet, over the past few decades, pioneering breakthroughs have gradually demystified these complexities, breathing life into the once-theoretical frameworks. Laboratories around the globe are now abuzz with attempts to translate the enigmatic behavior of particles into tangible technologies, making the ephemeral promises of quantum theories tangible.

One of the noteworthy milestones in this journey has been the development of quantum algorithms that capitalize on properties such as superposition and entanglement. Whereas classical algorithms rely on binary operations, quantum algorithms perform calculations across a multidimensional space. A prime example is Shor's algorithm, which shows exponential speedup for factoring large numbers—a breakthrough with profound implications for cryptography. In practical terms, this means quantum computers could, one day, render many current encryption schemes obsolete, necessitating a shift in how we think about digital security.

The practical integration of quantum mechanics into computing is not without its challenges. Overcoming issues like decoherence —the tendency of qubits to lose their quantum state due to environmental interference—and error rates remains a significant hurdle. Nevertheless, incremental advances in quantum error correction are steadily paving the way for more robust quantum systems. Laboratories at institutions such as the Massachusetts Institute of Technology (MIT) and companies like IBM and Google are spearheading this research, concerted in their efforts to make scalable, fault-tolerant quantum computers a reality.

To illustrate this interplay of science and pragmatism, consider the case of the joint venture between a leading global pharmaceutical company and a prominent quantum computing firm. By integrating quantum computing into their drug discovery process, they could simulate complex molecules much more efficiently than with classical computers. This collaboration has led to a notable reduction in time and cost associated with drug development, suggesting how quantum computing is not simply an academic exercise but a tool with transformative implications for industries across the spectrum.

As we advance deeper into the realm of quantum potential, we find ourselves at a critical juncture where burgeoning technologies promise to address constraints that have long hindered classical systems. This exploration paves the way towards the end of this chapter, guiding readers into a future where the possibilities seem as boundless as they are thrilling, anchoring our understanding in the promises and challenges just on the horizon.

As we conclude this foundational chapter, "Understanding Quantum Mechanics – From Einstein to Qubits," we step away from the early 20th-century revolutions that challenged our deepest scientific convictions and arrive at the nascent realm of quantum computing—an era that promises to redefine our technological landscape. We began by setting the stage with the visionary contributions of Einstein, Planck, and Bohr, whose groundbreaking ideas disrupted classical physics and seeded the quantum world with possibilities as vast and boundless as the universe itself.

The exploration of core principles like superposition and entanglement introduced you to the enigmatic yet alluring nature of quantum phenomena. By appreciating how a single particle can embody multiple states or how particles remain mysteriously interconnected across great distances, we've built the theoretical infrastructure necessary for understanding quantum computing's potential.

We've examined how the inherent constraints of traditional computing sparked the quest for quantum solutions, positioning qubits as the harbingers of this computational revolution. These powerful units of quantum information, operating beyond classic binary logic, promise untold computational feats and a new horizon of technological capabilities.

As we bridge these timeless scientific principles with cutting-edge computational innovation, it becomes increasingly apparent that we stand on the verge of technological breakthroughs that will dramatically reshape industries and redefine problem-solving approaches across domains.

In the chapters to come, we will delve deeper into the practical applications of this technology, illuminating how quantum computing is already beginning to impact areas from cryptography to artificial intelligence. Let this be not just a journey of understanding but one of imagination and foresight, as we continue to explore the quantum frontier, transforming curiosity into innovation and laying the groundwork for the tech revolution awaiting us just over the horizon.

CHAPTER 2: THE BIRTH OF QUANTUM COMPUTING

In the ever-evolving landscape of technological innovation, few realms capture the imagination quite like quantum computing. Its inception represents a radical departure from the familiar world of classical computers, where traditional bits give way to the enigmatic qubits of the quantum domain. This chapter, "The Birth of Quantum Computing," embarks on an enlightening journey to the origins and evolution of this transformative field, a journey that promises to unravel uncharted possibilities at the intersection of theory and reality.

Quantum computing's story is one of evolution from abstract quantum mechanics to tangible innovation that promises profound shifts in computational power and capability. We begin with "From Theory to Reality – The Genesis of Quantum Computing," setting the stage with an exploration of foundational ideas and visionary figures like Richard Feynman and David Deutsch. It is their pioneering theoretical frameworks that have made quantum computing not just a concept, but a conceivable paradigm shift from the limitations of classical computing, fueling a realm of potential once deemed science fiction.

As we navigate further into the chapter, "Groundbreaking Breakthroughs – The Dawn of a New Era" takes center stage. This subchapter unveils the seminal breakthroughs—the pioneering algorithms by minds like Peter Shor and Lov Grover—that illuminated the dawn of quantum potential. The discussion is punctuated by the rise of the qubit, the fundamental unit that elevates quantum computing above its classical predecessor. Readers are invited to witness the innovative spirit and intellectual rigor that have propelled quantum advancements into the spotlight, poised to revolutionize computation as we know it.

In "The Innovators and Their Contributions," attention turns to the architects of this nascent era—the brilliant individuals and forward-thinking institutions that have sculpted the quantum landscape. From the groundbreaking endeavors of Charles Bennett and Alain Aspect to the dynamic roles of behemoths like IBM and Google, this section spotlights the collaborative network of minds that fuels the engine of quantum progress.

Yet, to comprehend fully this technological leap requires understanding its departure from classical norms. "Quantum vs. Classical – Understanding the Differences" provides a crucial exposition of the intrinsic phenomena—such as superposition, entanglement, and wave-particle duality—that endow quantum systems with their distinctive capabilities. Through accessible insights and practical examples, we demystify how these quantum principles exponentially enhance computing efficiency and revolutionize problem-solving approaches.

As we conclude this chapter, "Setting the Stage – Preparing for Deeper Exploration" frames the current state of quantum computing and lays the groundwork for the journey ahead. Here, we explore the essential infrastructure and preparatory work necessary to propel quantum systems from experimental labs to mainstream utility, surmounting challenges toward broader adoption.

By weaving together history, breakthroughs, contributors, and foundational comparisons, "The Birth of Quantum Computing" invites you to explore the origins and trajectories of a field set to redefine the technological frontier. Join this journey into a realm where science and imagination converge, offering a glimpse into the computing revolution that lies just beyond the horizon.

From Theory to Reality – The Genesis of Quantum Computing

The realm of quantum computing owes its existence to a foundational branch of physics: quantum mechanics. Rooted in the exploration of subatomic phenomena, quantum mechanics challenges our conventional understanding of the physical world, presenting a universe where particles exist in multiple states simultaneously and influence one another instantaneously over vast distances. This subchapter seeks to unravel the intricate dance from theoretical musings to the emergent, tangible field of quantum computing.

Our journey begins in the mid-20th century, when quantum mechanics, with its curious tendencies and counterintuitive principles, began to lay the groundwork for what would eventually become quantum computing. Visionaries like Richard Feynman, renowned for his ability to elucidate the complexities of quantum physics through his innovative lectures and seminal papers, began contemplating the implications of a computer that harnessed quantum principles. In the 1980s, Feynman expressly articulated the potential of quantum computers, theorizing that classical computers were insufficient for simulating quantum systems. His insights into how quantum computers could mimic the intricacies of nature marked a pivotal moment in the conceptualization of quantum computing.

Parallel to Feynman's pioneering thoughts was another luminary, David Deutsch. His work formalized the concept of a universal quantum computer, capable of performing any calculation that classical computers could, but far more efficiently. Deutsch's introduction of the concept of quantum parallelism —a quantum computer's ability to process multiple possibilities simultaneously—foreshadowed the superior computational power these machines could offer. Together, Feynman and Deutsch catalyzed the theoretical speculation that served as a beacon for scientists and engineers in pursuit of a new computational frontier.

An illustrative example of quantum computing's transition from abstraction to practicality lies in IBM's early quantum research efforts. In the late 1990s, the team at IBM shattered previous limitations by building rudimentary quantum circuits, demonstrating quantum algorithms on a small scale. While these initial circuits were far from today's sophisticated machines, they represented a critical proof-of-concept, affirming that the principles articulated by Feynman and Deutsch could indeed be harnessed in a physical form.

To appreciate the leap from concept to application, consider the development of the nitrogen-vacancy (NV) center in diamonds. This innovative approach allows for the manipulation of quantum states at room temperature, presenting significant advantages over the cryogenic conditions many quantum systems require. The NV center has expanded the horizon for real-world quantum applications, such as incredibly precise sensing technologies, evidencing the practicality and versatility of quantum mechanics applied to computing.

As we bridge towards the next subchapter, we turn our gaze to the groundbreaking breakthroughs that further solidified quantum computing's relevance and viability. The groundbreaking theories debated and developed by Feynman, Deutsch, and their peers set the stage for the pivotal advancements that followed, revolutionizing our computational capabilities.

Practical Application:

Consider the role of quantum computing in modern cryptographic methods. The susceptibility of current encryption standards to quantum attacks necessitates new paradigms in data protection. Quantum computers, leveraging principles like Shor's algorithm, present a formidable challenge to traditional encryption; however, they simultaneously inspire the advent of quantum-resistant cryptography. This dual nature exemplifies how theoretical insights are not merely academic but critically influence present-day technological evolution. Thus, understanding the genesis of quantum computing elucidates not just how far we have come but how these innovations will continue to shape industries reliant on secure, efficient data management in the years ahead.

Groundbreaking Breakthroughs – The Dawn of a New Era

The journey of quantum computing from abstract theory to palpable reality is a tale of human ingenuity and breakthrough discoveries. It is a story that unfolds through paradigm-shifting milestones and the pioneering visionaries who engineered this technological marvel. In this subchapter, we navigate the milestones and the rich tapestry of breakthroughs that cast quantum computing into the limelight.

One cannot discuss quantum computing breakthroughs without highlighting the seminal contributions of Peter Shor. His 1994 algorithm, which efficiently factors large numbers, illustrated a quantum computer's theoretical ability to perform tasks beyond the scope of classical computers. This transformative application demonstrated how quantum computing could revolutionize fields like cryptography, which relies heavily on the difficulty of factorization as a security measure. Shor's algorithm marked quantum computing as a formidable force with the potential to redefine digital security.

Lov Grover further extended this frontier with his quantum search algorithm, optimizing the search process in unsorted databases. Grover's algorithm proved that quantum computing could execute specific tasks in a fraction of the time required by classical methods. This algorithm laid the foundation for tackling complex search and optimization problems, showcasing quantum computing's potential to solve real-world challenges across diverse domains, from database management to logistics.

Central to the quantum revolution is the concept of the qubit, which distinguishes quantum computers from their classical counterparts. Where classical computers use bits as the basic computing unit, encoding data as 0 or 1, quantum computers harness qubits, which exist in superposition. This allows them to encode data as both 0 and 1 simultaneously. The implications are profound: qubits can process multiple possibilities at once, exponentially increasing computational power and efficiency.

To visualize this, imagine the classic problem of solving a maze. A classical computer tackles this by exploring one path at a time until it finds the exit. A quantum computer, by leveraging superposition and entanglement, can theoretically assess all potential paths simultaneously, arriving at a solution with unprecedented speed. This intrinsic capability underpins quantum computing's potential to innovate across fields reliant on complex problem-solving.

Further solidifying this nascent era, prominent institutions and technology firms have embarked on efforts to harness and extend these breakthroughs into practical applications. For instance, Google's quantum processor Sycamore claimed quantum supremacy by performing a computational task in seconds that would take classical supercomputers millennia. This moment highlighted the tangible potential of quantum systems and set the stage for practical application and expansion.

A case study that encapsulates these successes can be found in the field of drug discovery. Traditional methods often involve immense data sets and computational challenges that can stretch for years. Quantum computing offers a new horizon, wherein simulations of molecular interactions—an overwhelming task for classical systems—become feasible. By simulating complex molecules and predicting their behavior, quantum computing has the potential to revolutionize pharmacology, leading to faster, more efficient drug development processes.

As the subchapter draws to a close, we pivot from these key achievements to the driving forces behind these advancements. Our exploration naturally transitions to the individuals and institutions—the architects of this quantum frontier—whose innovation and collaboration continue to propel the field to new heights. The coming section will delve into the stories of these innovators, offering insights into the human spirit and collaborative culture at the heart of quantum research.

The Innovators and Their Contributions

In the realm of quantum computing, progress is propelled by the relentless curiosity and pioneering spirit of individuals who dare to venture into the unknown. This subchapter aims to shine a spotlight on these innovators and their seminal contributions, offering insight into the personal and professional paths that have shaped the technological landscape.

Charles Bennett stands as a paragon of quantum experimentation and theory, exploring concepts like quantum cryptography and quantum teleportation. His work at IBM paved the way for practical quantum research, demonstrating that ideas once confined to theoretical discourse could find concrete application. Bennett's groundbreaking explorations into the thermodynamics of information not only influenced cryptography but also prodded the quantum field to reconsider the role of information theory in computing.

Similarly, Alain Aspect's revolutionary experiments with entangled photons at the University of Paris have been crucial. His trials provided empirical support for quantum entanglement, a cornerstone of quantum theory first proposed by Einstein, Podolsky, and Rosen. Aspect's work went beyond demonstrating entanglement's reality, highlighting its potential to challenge classical intuitions and create new approaches in computing and communications.

Beyond individual breakthroughs, leading institutions have fostered environments conducive to quantum advancements. IBM and Google have taken center stage, building scalable quantum systems that diminish the gap between experimental and computational realms. IBM's Quantum Experience platform, for instance, allows researchers and hobbyists alike to access quantum processors via the cloud, democratizing technology and fostering innovation. This initiative fosters a collaborative atmosphere reminiscent of open-source communities, where cross-pollination of ideas accelerates progress.

The story of Google and its 2019 "quantum supremacy" claim, where its quantum processor Sycamore allegedly performed a task unfeasible for classical machines, underscores the fierce competition and ambition driving quantum R&D. Despite debates on the supremacy claim's validity, the incident exemplifies the strategic push towards realistic quantum applications and galvanizes efforts across the tech landscape.

An illustrative case study emerges in the partnership between D-Wave Systems and Volkswagen. Recognizing quantum annealing's unique potential, Volkswagen leveraged D-Wave's quantum computer to optimize and refine traffic flow in challenging urban environments. The case highlights how industry players are beginning to implement quantum technologies in practical scenarios, offering a glimpse into a future where quantum solutions can optimize complex logistical challenges.

As we analyze the human element behind quantum computing's rapid development, it is imperative to understand that these technological strides result from both individual ingenuity and collaborative synergy. With a robust foundation now established by these trailblazers, we transition into the next subchapter, where a nuanced comparison between quantum and classical paradigms awaits to further enrich our comprehension of their respective roles and capabilities.

Quantum vs. Classical – Understanding the Differences

In the digital universe we inhabit, the distinction between quantum and classical computing is akin to comparing two vastly different worlds, each with its own set of rules and potential. The classical computers that have been the bedrock of technological growth for decades operate on binary systems—zeros and ones. In contrast, quantum computing enters a realm where data are no longer constrained to a binary existence. Here, we explore foundational concepts that define quantum computing and differentiate it from classical paradigms.

At the heart of quantum computing are phenomena like superposition and entanglement. Superposition allows quantum bits, or qubits, to exist simultaneously in multiple states—both zero and one. Imagine flipping a coin not just landing in heads or tails, but existing in a state of both heads and tails at once until observed. This property exponentially increases the computational power, as a quantum computer with just a few qubits can store and process vast amounts of data concurrently.

Take, for example, a complex problem like molecular simulation. Classical computers would approach this task by calculating probabilities in sequence, an endeavor that could take years. Quantum computers, leveraging superposition, could process numerous possibilities simultaneously, accelerating calculations drastically.

Entanglement, another pivotal concept, refers to the interconnection between qubits. When qubits become entangled, the state of one immediately influences the state of another, regardless of distance. This feature facilitates unprecedented information transmission speeds, conjuring brewing possibilities in secure communications and data encryption.

A tangible demonstration of these quantum principles can be seen in quantum cryptography. Consider a citywide network where businesses rely on secure data sharing. Classical cryptographic methods are time-consuming and subject to hacking attempts. Quantum computing introduces a revolutionary alternative: quantum key distribution, or QKD. This method ensures secure communication by detecting eavesdropping through changes in entangled qubits, guaranteeing data integrity and privacy with unmatched certainty.

These quantum phenomena evoke comparisons with classical systems—a single classical bit can only represent one state at a time, while measuring a qubit requires embracing uncertainty, a paradigm shift that symbolizes the broader differences in processing efficiency. The parallelism in quantum computing harnesses the ability to perform numerous computations at the same time, a quality inherently absent in classical algorithms.

To appreciate the real-world implications, consider the realm of artificial intelligence. Classical computers might take years to optimize vast neural networks for complex learning tasks due to sequential processing limits. Quantum computing can revolutionize this domain by performing concurrent operations, refining AI capabilities more rapidly and effectively.

Transitioning from this examination of core quantum

phenomena, the subsequent subchapter will explore the practical foundations necessary for operationalizing quantum computers, setting the stage for future innovations within this dynamic field. As we move forward, consider the potential efficiencies and security enhancements that these quantum principles afford, already reshaping industries in substantive ways.

Setting the Stage – Preparing for Deeper Exploration

Quantum computing stands poised on the brink of extraordinary advancements, akin to the dawn of the digital age that reshaped society in the late 20th century. As with any nascent technology, the pathway to a mature, universally integrated quantum ecosystem is paved with both remarkable opportunities and formidable challenges. In this subchapter, we embark on a journey to understand the current landscape of quantum computing, setting a firm foundation for the discussions that will follow in subsequent chapters. By illuminating the infrastructure requirements—encompassing hardware, algorithms, and the necessary supportive technologies—we aim to paint a comprehensive picture of what it takes to actualize the potential of quantum computing.

The development of quantum hardware represents one of the most significant hurdles in transitioning quantum computing from theory to reality. Unlike classical systems, which rely on bits, quantum computers harness the mysterious and powerful qubit. These qubits, capable of existing in multiple states simultaneously, require extremely delicate conditions to maintain coherence. The current state of quantum hardware often revolves around maintaining these qubits at cryogenic temperatures within highly controlled environments—a feat that stretches the limits of engineering and material science. Companies like D-Wave, Rigetti, and IBM are at the forefront of this quest, each deploying unique methodologies to tackle these challenges and pushing the boundaries of what is technologically feasible.

Equally pivotal to the progress in quantum computing is the development of sophisticated quantum algorithms that leverage the unique properties of quantum states. Shor's algorithm, which efficiently factors large numbers, and Grover's algorithm, offering quadratic speed-ups in unsorted database searches, are but a glimpse into the computational prowess quantum algorithms could offer. However, translating theoretical advantages into practical, error-free quantum computing applications demands continued algorithmic innovation and error-correction strategies. This necessitates a new breed of thinkers—quantum software developers with the acumen to navigate and innovate within this complex computational paradigm.

As we look to the supportive technologies that will buttress quantum computing, we find ourselves contemplating an expansive network of capabilities. Quantum simulation, for instance, has emerged as an invaluable tool for testing theoretical models and understanding complex quantum phenomena. Moreover, technologies related to quantum communications and cryptography are quickly evolving, promising heightened security protocols that could redefine data protection standards across industries.

The journey to widespread quantum computing adoption also requires significant collaborative efforts across academia, industry, and government. Public-private partnerships and international collaborations are materializing, aimed at fostering breakthroughs, sharing knowledge, and addressing regulatory challenges. Funding and resources from entities like the European Union's Quantum Flagship and the U.S. National Quantum Initiative underscore the concerted effort being made globally to pave the way for quantum advancements.

To ground these concepts in the tangible progress being made, let us consider the Quantum Innovation Lab at Google. This cutting-edge research hub exemplifies how concerted efforts and resources can catalyze advancements in quantum technology. By creating an environment that nurtures pioneering research, Google has been able to demonstrate quantum supremacy —a milestone where a quantum computer outperformed the best classical computers at a specific task. This achievement underscores the potential of quantum technology to address complex computing problems previously thought insurmountable.

As we navigate the unfolding landscape of quantum technology, understanding its potential and its hurdles prepares us for meaningful exploration into its future applications and deepens our appreciation of its transformative promise. As we move forward, the intricacies of integrating quantum computing into everyday technology will become clearer, setting the stage for further revelations and innovations discussed in later chapters.

As we close this chapter on the birth of quantum computing, we're reminded that even the most transformative revolutions begin as whispers in the corridors of theoretical musings. Our journey traversed the foundational landscape laid by quantum mechanics, illuminated by visionaries like Richard Feynman and David Deutsch, whose intellectual bravery sketched the first blueprints of quantum dominion. The advancements celebrated here—the pioneering algorithms of Shor and Grover and the monumental introduction of the qubit—serve as both testament and tribute to the relentless ingenuity igniting this new era.

In recognizing the stalwart contributions of innovators such as

Charles Bennett and Alain Aspect, alongside the institutional might of companies like IBM and Google, it becomes evident that quantum progress is not the fruit of solitary endeavor but a symphony of collaborative ambition. Their shared efforts have set the stage for a paradigm where the surreal nature of quantum phenomena renders new frontiers attainable.

Yet, the duality of quantum versus classical computing challenges and inspires us with its complexity and promise. As these seemingly disparate worlds collide and converge, we find a departure from linear logic and embrace a future of expansive computational horizons. This chapter compels us not only to understand these theoretical constructs but to envision their tangible impacts on our world.

As we transition to the next chapter, consider the vast possibilities that quantum technology affords—how each breakthrough is a stepping stone toward unprecedented innovations. Equipped with an appreciation for both its enigmatic nature and practical potential, we now move forward, prepared to explore the intricacies of quantum algorithms and their real-world applications. Continue with a sense of curiosity and determination, for the path ahead holds answers—and new questions—in equal measure.

CHAPTER 3:
CRYPTOGRAPHY AND
QUANTUM SECURITY

I n a world increasingly defined by digital interconnectivity, cryptography stands as the invisible guardian of our most sensitive information. It weaves through every facet of our digital existence, underpinning the security that allows us to interact, transact, and trust in this virtual age. However, as we stand at the threshold of the quantum era, the very bedrock of our digital security is poised for potential upheaval. In Chapter 3 of "Quantum Frontier: Demystifying the Next Tech Revolution," we delve into the intricate realm of cryptography and quantum security, traversing the fascinating narrative of how quantum computing springs both peril and promise upon the cryptographic landscape.

The chapter opens with an essential exploration of the foundational techniques in traditional cryptography. We illuminate the significance of methods like public key infrastructure and symmetric key algorithms. These time-honored systems have long been the stalwarts of digital protection. Yet, as our narrative unfolds, we unearth the vulnerabilities intrinsic to these classical encryption techniques.

The relentless march of technological advancement now nears a pivotal threat—quantum computing. Here, we set the stage to reveal why new cryptographic solutions are not merely desirable but indispensable, given this looming shift.

Transitioning into the realm where quantum computing threatens these classical bastions, we decode the complexities surrounding algorithms like Shor's algorithm. This quantum capability poses a formidable challenge, presenting an ability to unravel cryptographic codes once thought impenetrable. In an accessible yet comprehensive manner, we delineate how this quantum prowess threatens to render traditional encryption methods obsolete and explore the vast implications this realization holds for global cybersecurity infrastructures.

In response to such existential threats, the chapter charts a course into the burgeoning world of quantum-resistant cryptography. This new frontier seeks to outpace the capabilities of quantum decryption with innovative approaches and robust defenses. We delve into a parallel universe of lattice-based cryptography and hash-based signatures, capturing the pulse of ongoing research and development. The promise of these emerging advancements speaks to a future where quantum challenges are met with equal technological resilience.

The narrative then elegantly shifts toward quantum key distribution (QKD), an evocative intersection of science and innovation. This groundbreaking method fosters a new paradigm of security through the principles of quantum mechanics themselves. With illustrative clarity, we explore how protocols like BB84 revolutionize secure communication, thwarting eavesdroppers with a simplicity that seems conjured from science fiction.

Finally, this chapter concludes by grounding our journey in the real world, highlighting practical applications and the collaborative undertakings essential to fortifying our digital defenses against quantum incursions. From finance to telecommunications, the path forward demands concerted efforts from international bodies, governments, and private sectors alike. It is here, in envisioning the cybersecurity landscape of tomorrow, that readers come to appreciate the transformative power of quantum innovations.

As we navigate this chapter, we engage not just in understanding but in preparing for the transformative revolution at our doorstep —one where the theoretical mettle of quantum magic is tested against the stakes of global security. Through this lens, the chapter serves as both guide and guardian, demystifying the quantum challenge and inspiring confidence in a world where science and security continue to coalesce in ever-surprising ways.

The Foundations of Cryptography and Its Vulnerabilities

Cryptography sits at the heart of digital security, a discipline as old as writing itself, emerging from the need to shield information from prying eyes. Our journey through its labyrinth begins with an exploration of the foundational tools: public key infrastructure and symmetric key algorithms, which have steadfastly protected our digital secrets for decades.

Symmetric key algorithms such as the Advanced Encryption Standard (AES) have long been the sentinel of secure communications. They use a single key for both encryption and decryption, a methodology reminiscent of ancient ciphers that relied on pre-arranged keywords. While efficient, the logistical challenge of distributing and managing these keys securely without interception or duplication has persistently dogged this approach, exposing a critical vulnerability.

Public key infrastructure (PKI), introduced in the 1970s, revolutionized cryptography by eliminating the need for prior secure key exchange. Through the ingenious use of paired keys—

public and private—users could encrypt messages with a public key that only an associated private key could decrypt. The RSA algorithm, a stalwart of PKI, relies heavily on the arduous task of factoring large semiprime numbers, a mathematical problem that proved insurmountable for classical computers.

Yet, every fortress has its Achilles' heel. With symmetric systems, the mere exposure of the key spells catastrophe. In PKI, the indomitable assumption of computationally infeasible factoring is vulnerable to the quantum storms brewing on the horizon. For instance, the impending reality of Shor's algorithm, which allows for efficient factoring, casts a shadow over RSA's safety, prodding the cryptographic community to rethink their defenses.

These vulnerabilities are not theoretical musings but practical concerns. Consider a medical facility that relies on classical encryption to protect patient records. An adversarial breach through quantum means could unlock sensitive data, prompting a healthcare disaster. Such scenarios amplify the bona fide necessity for advancing beyond traditional protections.

Moreover, consider the realm of financial transactions. Banks universally depend on cryptography to secure millions of online exchanges each minute. In a quantum-infused future, the exposure of encryption keys could unravel this intricate web, leading to staggering breaches. The stakes are not merely digital but profoundly economic and personal.

To appreciate the compelling need for development in cryptography, one must recognize the remarkable reliability yet inherent frailty underscoring these traditional methods. Their evolution, driven by the accelerating pace of technological advancement, is not just advisable; it is imperative. This urgency propels us toward the threshold of a quantum era, where new paradigms promise to redefine cybersecurity's contours and standards.

As we segue into examining the incipient quantum threats

challenging these classical bastions, consider this real-world application: During the advent of WWII, cryptographic breakthroughs such as the enigma machine underscored the perils and potential of code-making. Revisiting this pivotal episode through a modern lens invites us to explore the vast expanse where quantum capabilities threaten to unravel our digital fortresses, compelling us to forge a new order of cryptographic resilience.

The Quantum Threat to Classical Encryption

In the realm of cryptography, classical encryption methods such as RSA and ECC have long provided the spine of our digital security infrastructure. These methods typically rely on the computational difficulty of problems like factoring large numbers or solving discrete logarithms. Historically, these problems have been considered infeasible to crack using classical computers within a practical timeframe. However, the advent of quantum computing threatens to overturn this foundational principle.

At the heart of this quantum threat lies Shor's algorithm, an extraordinary computational method that allows a sufficiently powerful quantum computer to factorize large numbers exponentially faster than classical computers can. In practical terms, this translates to a looming obsolescence for traditional encryption schemes, as a quantum computer running Shor's algorithm could decrypt data protected by RSA in a fraction of the time once deemed impossible.

To illustrate, consider the case of secure internet communication, which heavily relies on RSA encryption to protect sensitive data such as online banking information. The strength of RSA has traditionally been its reliance on large key sizes, which classical computers struggle to break. However, with quantum computers on the horizon capable of running Shor's algorithm efficiently, the security offered by these large keys dwindles. Imagine a world where an adversary with access to a quantum computer could eavesdrop on encrypted communications, potentially accessing personal financial details or classified government information.

The magnitude of the quantum threat extends beyond just data decryption. It threatens to undermine the very trust in digital systems that underpin our modern society. Without robust encryption, the integrity of financial transactions, the confidentiality of communications, and even the security of critical infrastructure could be at risk.

Real-world implications of this threat are already being acknowledged in sectors highly sensitive to data security breaches. Financial institutions, aware of the potential devastation a quantum attack could unleash, are actively investing in research to develop quantum-safe cryptographic solutions. This proactive approach is mirrored across governments and global security agencies, underscoring the necessity of evolving our cryptographic defenses in tandem with technological advancements.

One notable example is the recent collaboration between significant financial hubs and tech innovators, aimed at testing quantum-resistant algorithms in real-world scenarios. These pilot programs simulate quantum attacks to assess vulnerabilities, providing valuable insights that inform the development of robust countermeasures.

As we pivot towards quantum resilience, understanding the precise nature of the quantum threat is paramount. The next frontier lies in post-quantum cryptography, where the development of new cryptographic algorithms promises to fortify our digital ecosystem against the capabilities of quantum computing. This exploration continues into the next subchapter, as we delve into the pioneering field of post-quantum cryptography and its pivotal role in ensuring the future security of our cyber infrastructure.

Quantum-Resistant Cryptography
– Building the Future of
Safe Communication

In the dawn of the quantum era, the cryptographic world finds itself at a pivotal crossroads. Classical encryption, like the stalwart RSA and the ubiquitous AES, has long protected our secrets, assets, and infrastructure. However, with quantum computers looming on the horizon, capable of solving complex mathematical problems intractable for classical machines, the future of these cryptographic bastions is uncertain. Enter post-quantum cryptography: the promise of cryptographic safety in the age of quantum computation.

The very premises of post-quantum cryptography rest upon mathematical problems that remain resistant to both classical and quantum algorithms. Lattice-based cryptography, for example, focuses on the hardness of certain lattice problems, which appear immune to the efficiencies offered by quantum computing. These systems leverage the complexity of navigating multidimensional lattices, providing a robust defense even under the scrutiny of a quantum adversary. Similarly, hash-based signatures offer another layer of security, utilizing cryptographic hash functions that maintain resilience against quantum attack vectors.

Transitioning from theoretical exploration to tangible application involves a myriad of challenges. Implementing quantum-resistant algorithms into current systems requires rigorous testing and a reevaluation of existing infrastructure. Consider the financial sector, where milliseconds in encryption can translate to monumental shifts in economic flow. The integration of post-quantum cryptographic solutions into such time-sensitive environments entails strategic collaboration across multiple stakeholders, including cryptographers, software engineers, and regulatory bodies.

The ongoing global efforts towards standardizing post-quantum cryptography further emphasize the urgency. The National Institute of Standards and Technology (NIST) has been at the forefront, fostering innovation and evaluating submissions to define new standards for public-key cryptography. These initiatives serve a dual purpose: they propel research and innovation while ensuring that the technology remains accessible and universally applicable.

As we navigate these uncharted waters, consider the real-world scenario of the telecommunications industry, where the secure exchange of information is paramount. One notable case study involves a leading international telecom company deploying lattice-based cryptography to protect client data from quantum threats. Through partnerships with academia and government agencies, it has not only fortified its communication infrastructure against potential quantum attacks but also set a standard for others in the industry.

In embracing quantum-resistant cryptography, we are not merely reacting to a looming crisis but proactively shaping the landscape of secure communication in the digital age. By implementing these advanced cryptographic measures, industries can safeguard their assets and preserve the integrity of their information systems against both current and future threats. This transformative journey towards quantum resilience underpins the very fabric of tomorrow's secure communication frameworks —an exciting precursor to further exploration in quantum key distribution methods, where the marvels of quantum mechanics offer new paradigms in cybersecurity.

Quantum Key Distribution – A New Paradigm of Security

In the ever-evolving landscape of digital security, Quantum Key Distribution (QKD) emerges as a groundbreaking paradigm that harnesses the stranger-than-fiction principles of quantum mechanics to achieve unprecedented levels of communication security. At its core, QKD enables two parties to share encryption keys with absolute confidentiality, sidestepping the risks of traditional distribution methods. This subchapter delves into the intriguing mechanics of QKD, illuminating the pathway to a future where intercepted communications could become a relic of the past.

QKD operates on the counterintuitive but scientifically proven principles of quantum physics, where particles exist in multiple states until observed. This phenomenon, famously captured in the act of "wavefunction collapse," implies that any attempt at eavesdropping on a quantum channel unavoidably alters the state of the quantum particles involved, thereby revealing the intrusion. Among the most renowned protocols in QKD is the BB84 protocol, introduced by Charles Bennett and Gilles Brassard in 1984. Leveraging the properties of polarized photons, the BB84 protocol ensures that any anomalous attempt to intercept or measure these photons results in detectable disturbances, alerting legitimate users to potential breaches.

As interest in QKD has surged, practical applications have begun to surface across various sectors. Consider the finance industry, where the stakes for secure transactions are nothing short of existential. A leading European bank recently invested in a pilot QKD network, connecting its major financial hubs via a web of fiber optic cables capable of transmitting quantum-encrypted data. Early trials have demonstrated remarkable resilience against interception, offering a glimmer of hope for an industry constantly under the siege of cyber threats. By implementing QKD, the bank not only enhances its security architecture but also sets a precedent for other financial institutions globally considering similar advancements.

The transition towards widespread deployment of QKD is not without challenges. The current infrastructure requires substantial adaptations to accommodate the sensitive nature of quantum signals, typically necessitating enhanced fiber optic networks or even dedicated satellite links for longer distance communications. Furthermore, the need for synchronization between compatible quantum devices underscores the necessity for a new kind of inter-network standardization, as crucial in our quantum future as TCP/IP is today for existing digital communications.

Perhaps more intriguing is the potential for QKD to integrate with other quantum technologies, laying the groundwork for a comprehensive quantum internet. Here, quantum nodes could ensure secure connections worldwide, offering real-time security that not only protects data in transit but also gives rise to novel applications previously deemed infeasible. Imagine, for instance, a healthcare system underpinned by quantum networks, where patient data flows securely between practitioners, creating a seamless, safeguarded tapestry of personalized healthcare delivery.

One pioneering example comes from the burgeoning field of telecommunications. A consortium led by a major Asian telecommunications firm has launched a city-wide QKD testbed, encompassing both fiber and free-space communication channels. This initiative seeks to rigorously test the reliability of quantum encryption across various environmental conditions and urban landscapes. Preliminary results are encouraging, demonstrating the feasibility of scalable quantum networks capable of fortifying national security infrastructures against mounting cyber threats. The project's ambition extends beyond mere novelty, envisioning a resilient digital ecosystem where the very thought of undetected surveillance or data theft becomes obsolete.

As we transition from this foundational exploration of Quantum Key Distribution, the journey into cryptographic innovation is far from complete. In the next subchapter, we will probe into the real-world applications and trajectories that quantum security promises, examining how industries are navigating these technological waters and forging ahead into a future where trust and confidentiality are inextricably bound to the quantum world.

Real-World Applications and the Path Ahead for Quantum Security

As we navigate the rapidly evolving landscape of quantum security, the implications for real-world applications become both captivating and urgent. This subchapter delves into how industries are adapting to quantum advances, highlighting the tangible steps being taken to defend against quantum-enabled threats and harness the power of quantum technologies.

In the financial sector, institutions are leading the charge toward quantum readiness. As transactions increasingly move online, the security of these exchanges becomes paramount. Banks are piloting solutions that integrate quantum-resistant cryptographic algorithms to safeguard sensitive data from future quantum attacks. For example, JP Morgan Chase is collaborating with IBM on quantum cloud initiatives, aiming to develop secure digital currencies that can withstand quantum decryption attempts. This initiative highlights a proactive approach, where businesses are not merely reacting to potential threats but preparing for an inevitable quantum era.

Meanwhile, the telecommunications industry plays a pivotal role in building robust quantum-safe infrastructures. The deployment of quantum key distribution (QKD) technology across communication networks illustrates this proactive defense strategy. Companies like China Mobile have explored QKD to protect their vast communication networks, successfully implementing QKD on selected routes to guarantee secure transmission of data. These cases underscore the industry-wide urgency to adopt new security protocols that ensure safe communication channels in a post-quantum world.

Government agencies also face the daunting task of upgrading national security frameworks to incorporate quantum technologies. The European Union, for instance, has launched the Quantum Flagship program, allocating considerable resources toward nurturing quantum research from theoretical foundations to commercial viability. Within this initiative, multi-national collaborations aim to develop quantum-safe cryptographic standards, setting benchmarks that will guide future security policies on a global scale.

The path toward quantum security is further empowered by collaborations between private sectors, academic institutions, and international bodies. These partnerships fuel innovation and facilitate the sharing of best practices across borders. A notable example is the alliance between the National Institute of Standards and Technology (NIST) in the United States and academic researchers worldwide. This collaboration is pivotal in vetting and standardizing post-quantum cryptographic algorithms, fostering a resilient digital ecosystem capable of withstanding quantum threats.

To illustrate the transformative potential of quantum security, consider the integration of quantum technologies in healthcare. As patient data increasingly shifts to digital platforms, ensuring the confidentiality and integrity of this information is critical. Researchers at the University of Geneva are exploring QKD to secure the transmission of medical records between hospitals and research facilities. This project highlights how quantum security can protect sensitive information from falling into the wrong hands while maintaining accessibility for authorized personnel.

As we move forward in this new quantum paradigm, every

industry must remain vigilant and adaptive, embracing the technological shifts necessary to safeguard their operations. The collaborative efforts and groundbreaking partnerships currently being forged set a precedent for how we must approach the future of digital security in a quantum world. With practical applications already underway and the ongoing pursuit of quantum-safe protocols, organizations can be reassured that they are not alone in this journey of adaptation and resilience.

As we conclude this pivotal chapter on Cryptography and Quantum Security, we've traversed the intricate landscape that defines the bedrock of digital security today. We've acknowledged the resilience and vulnerabilities of traditional cryptographic methods, recognizing their imminent obsolescence as quantum computing looms on the horizon. Through our exploration of Shor's algorithm, we've comprehended the profound implications quantum advancements pose to prevailing systems like RSA, bringing us face-to-face with the critical need for quantum-resistant solutions.

These solutions, the groundwork of future communication security, are emerging brightly on the quantum horizon. From lattice-based cryptography to hash-based signatures, innovation is paving the way for a safer digital future, albeit amidst intricate challenges and the necessity for global standardization. Moreover, the advent of Quantum Key Distribution introduces a transformative dimension to security protocols, utilizing the very fabric of quantum mechanics to outmaneuver eavesdroppers.

The chapter's insights into real-world applications reveal an exciting trajectory for global industries, emphasizing the collaborative endeavors needed to fortify our cybersecurity infrastructure against quantum threats. As we stand at the threshold of unprecedented change, it's clear that adaptability and proactive innovation will be key in transitioning to this new era.

As we move forward to the next chapter, we will delve deeper into the broader implications of quantum advancements across various industry sectors, exploring how these technological leaps will reshape not only security but the very fabric of our societal architecture. Empowered with knowledge and inspired by possibility, we journey onward, equipped to transform theoretical insights into practical applications and confident in our ability to navigate the quantum frontier.

CHAPTER 4:
REVOLUTIONIZING
DRUG DISCOVERY AND
PHARMACOLOGY

In the ever-evolving landscape of drug discovery and pharmacology, we stand on the brink of a profound transformation driven by the pioneering domain of quantum computing. As we embark on this chapter's journey, we unlock the door to a realm where computational power surges beyond present-day boundaries, promising to redefine how we perceive and conduct drug discovery forever.

Imagine a world where the staggering complexity of molecular interactions can be deciphered with unprecedented precision and speed. This world is inching closer, thanks to the advent of quantum technology, which holds the key to solving molecular conundrums that classical computing has long struggled with. In the opening subchapter, "The Quantum Promise in Pharmacology," we set the stage for this revolution. We delve into the transformative potential that quantum algorithms harbor, paving the way for accelerated drug development, faster lead identification, and enhanced efficacy prediction. The vision we explore suggests a future where pharmacology is not just reshaped but redefined by the capabilities of quantum computing.

Our exploration deepens as we enter "Computational Chemistry and Quantum Algorithms," where the intricate workings of quantum computing within this field are unraveled. Here, we decode algorithms such as the Variational Quantum Eigensolver and Quantum Approximate Optimization Algorithm, demonstrating how they transcend traditional approaches. These groundbreaking algorithms bring clarity to complex molecular structures, enabling us to comprehend chemical interactions in novel ways, enhancing efficiency in bringing concepts to life as viable pharmaceutical products.

What follows is a vivid transition from theory to practice in "Case Studies in Quantum-Assisted Drug Discovery." This section animates the promising prospects discussed, offering tangible insights into current pioneering projects where quantum computing has already made significant impacts. Collaborations between pharmaceuticals and tech innovators are highlighted, showcasing groundbreaking case studies with detailed outcomes that illustrate the transformative benefits this technology is beginning to deliver.

Of course, no revolution is without its hurdles. "Overcoming Challenges and Technical Barriers" anchors our narrative in the realm of real-world challenges and limitations. We confront the technical barriers that still pose significant roadblocks, such as quantum decoherence and hardware constraints. This candid discussion balances the optimism of quantum's potential with a pragmatic look at the work still required to harness it fully, reflecting on the inventive solutions being developed to overcome these hurdles.

Finally, we peer into the "Future Landscape of Quantum-Driven Pharmacology." This concluding subchapter offers a compelling vision of personalized medicine, driven by quantum's capabilities to simulate individual patient profiles dynamically. In contemplating this speculative future, we bridge today's advancements with tomorrow's possibilities, inviting readers to envision a landscape where quantum computing becomes the backbone of tailored therapeutics.

Join us as we delve into this revolutionary narrative, illuminating the potential of quantum computing to forever alter the fields of drug discovery and pharmacology. With every page, we not only uncover the burgeoning capabilities at our fingertips but also inspire a future where the frontiers of science are continually expanded.

The Quantum Promise in Pharmacology

Embarking on the journey to understand the transformative potential of quantum computing in pharmacology necessitates an appreciation of the profound shifts it heralds in the landscape of drug discovery. At its core, quantum computing possesses the remarkable capacity to tackle and solve the knottiest of molecular conundrums that classical computers find insurmountable. This technological alchemy, driven by quantum algorithms, holds the promise of revolutionizing the precision and speed of drug development processes.

To fully grasp the promise of quantum computing in pharmacology, we must first consider its ability to perform molecular simulations with unparalleled accuracy. These simulations, critical to drug discovery, involve predicting the interaction between molecules—information that guides scientists in identifying promising candidates for therapeutic development. Quantum computers, due to their innate ability to exist in multiple states simultaneously, can process vast amounts of information exponentially faster than classical computers, opening new avenues for research and discovery.

In the realm of drug discovery, this quantum advantage translates to faster lead identification. Identifying promising compounds that could serve as the basis for new drugs is an arduous task, traditionally demanding significant time and computational resources. Quantum computing streamlines this process, enabling researchers to sift through immense data sets swiftly to pinpoint molecules with the highest likelihood of success, revolutionizing lead generation in drug development.

Additionally, quantum computing promises enhanced efficacy prediction—the ability to foresee how effective a drug will be, even before it is put through rigorous testing. Quantum models can simulate molecular interactions at an atomistic level with unprecedented precision, allowing scientists to foresee potential issues and refine drug candidates early in the development pipeline. This predictive prowess not only accelerates the drug discovery process but also markedly increases the chances of success in subsequent clinical trials.

To illustrate the burgeoning capabilities of quantum computing in pharmacology, consider a scenario involving a major pharmaceutical firm. Faced with the challenge of developing a novel antiviral drug, the firm leverages quantum computing to assess a library of tens of thousands of molecular structures. Through quantum simulations, they rapidly zero in on a small subset of molecules that not only show promise in binding effectively to the virus but also pass initial safety assessments. This quantum-assisted process reduces the traditional timeline from concept to candidate selection by years.

In a practical case, a collaboration between a leading biotech company and a quantum computing pioneer serves as a testament to the power of quantum promise in pharmacology. By integrating quantum computing into their research workflows, they managed to expedite the discovery of a candidate for a rare neurological condition, drastically cutting down the preliminary research phase from what usually takes years to mere months. This collaborative effort underscores how quantum computing is not just a theoretical prospect but a game-changing force redefining pharmacological frontiers.

As we transition to exploring the intricate mechanics of how quantum algorithms are utilized in computational chemistry, it becomes crucial to understand the technical underpinnings that make such leaps in drug discovery possible. The following subchapter delves deeper into the specifics of these algorithms, detailing their functionality and demonstrating their superiority over traditional methods in unraveling the complexities of molecular interactions.

Computational Chemistry and Quantum Algorithms

In the intricate dance of drug discovery, computational chemistry acts as the pivotal choreographer, orchestrating a symphony between molecules and prospective pharmaceuticals. It is here, within the microscopic theatre of atoms and bonds, that quantum computing begins to redefine the narrative. By combining the precision of quantum algorithms with the vast complexity of chemical interactions, we find ourselves at the dawn of a new era for pharmacology—one where previously insurmountable challenges are met with innovative solutions.

Quantum algorithms such as the Variational Quantum Eigensolver (VQE) and the Quantum Approximate Optimization Algorithm (QAOA) serve as the linchpins in this transformation. VQE, for instance, is designed to find the lowest energy state of a quantum system, which is crucial when modeling molecular structures. By harnessing quantum superposition and entanglement, VQE offers computational chemists the ability to simulate complex molecules with an accuracy and speed unattainable by classical means. This empowerment transcends the classical bottleneck of approximation errors that often plague traditional computational methods.

Consider the molecular structure of penicillin—one of the most celebrated discoveries in pharmaceutical history. Its discovery and subsequent mass production transformed medicine, yet the path from identification to clinical use was riddled with obstacles, including the inability to computationally model its full molecular structure due to technological constraints of that era. Fast forward to the present, quantum computing holds the potential to simulate not just penicillin but also molecules exponentially more complex, such as macromolecular proteins involved in Alzheimer's disease or intricate HIV proteins. These simulations are pivotal for understanding binding sites, stability, and reactivity—key factors in effective drug design and synthesis.

In practical terms, pharmaceutical companies are beginning to test the capabilities of quantum computing within their R&D frameworks. A notable example is the ongoing partnership between IBM and major pharmaceutical firms like Pfizer, where they're deploying VQE to explore the dynamics of potential drug interactions at a subatomic level. By accurately predicting molecular behavior and stability, these quantum simulations yield data that guide chemists in the design of more effective and safer compounds, theoretically reducing the timeline from conception to market approval.

However, the journey from computational possibility to actual application requires a robust understanding of the quantum-classical interface. Quantum hardware, though rapidly evolving, necessitates collaboration between quantum experts and chemists to integrate insights seamlessly into the drug discovery pipeline. This collaborative approach ensures that quantum algorithms not only complement but enhance existing computational frameworks, providing researchers with a multidimensional toolkit.

As the pharmaceutical industry begins to adapt to this quantum revolution, it becomes essential to gain proficiency in these emergent technologies. Real-life scenarios exemplify this convergence; for instance, in 2022, several biotech startups began leveraging QAOA for developing cancer therapies tailored to suppress specific mutations, significantly improving targeted treatment precision.

Transitioning from concept to application, one particular case surmounts the theoretical into the practical—an endeavor involving Harvard University and Biogen. Together, they have utilized VQE to simulate the binding efficiency of novel molecules against enzymes implicated in neurodegenerative diseases. While still in nascent stages, this project lays the groundwork for clinical trials that could see compounds designed in silico enter the in vitro phase, guided precisely by quantum-generated data.

Thus, as we broaden our understanding of these algorithms, we edge closer to a reality where computational chemistry —fortified by quantum insights—complements and enhances classical approaches, fostering a robust, dynamic methodology for drug discovery. In the subsequent subchapter, we will witness these theoretical advancements materialize through a series of detailed case studies, shedding light on how quantum-assisted drug discovery is already reshaping the pharmaceutical landscape today.

Case Studies in Quantum-Assisted Drug Discovery

As we venture into the heart of revolutionized discovery in drug development, it becomes imperative to pivot from theory to practice. Real-world case studies illuminate the profound impact that quantum computing is beginning to have within the pharmacology landscape. In doing so, these cases not only enliven our theoretical understanding but also provide a window into the concrete transformations underway in the field.

One of the pioneering endeavors that demonstrates the power of quantum computing is the collaboration between IBM's Quantum division and biotech company, Alán Laboratories. In a groundbreaking initiative, Alán Laboratories sought to apply quantum computing to enhance their antimicrobial resistance research. Traditional methods of exploring the vast chemical space for potential drug candidates were proving to be time-consuming and often yielded suboptimal results. However, by leveraging IBM's quantum capabilities, Alán Laboratories was able to utilize the Variational Quantum Eigensolver to simulate complex molecular interactions with unprecedented accuracy. This collaboration accelerated the identification of potential lead compounds, which, in turn, significantly reduced the time frame for initial drug candidate selection.

In another notable project, collaboration between Google AI Quantum and the pharmaceutical giant GlaxoSmithKline (GSK) marked a pivotal shift in cancer drug discovery. The use of Google's quantum computers allowed for the exploration of novel drug formulations aimed at combating drug resistance in cancer treatments. The Quantum Approximate Optimization Algorithm (QAOA) was instrumental in performing highly complex simulations of protein-drug interactions. These simulations facilitated the identification of binding sites that were previously overlooked using classical methods. This breakthrough enabled GSK to refine their development processes, yielding compounds with higher efficacy rates and opening new avenues for clinical trial exploration.

Such collaborations are not limited to large, well-funded entities. Cambridge Quantum Computing has collaborated with the startup BioQuant, aiming to democratize access to quantum computing in drug discovery. Through their efforts, BioQuant was able to explore quantum machine learning algorithms to predict the pharmacokinetics of newly designed molecules. By breaking down the complex correlations between molecular structures and their dynamic processes in the body, quantum computing enabled BioQuant to enhance both the speed and quality of drug design, hosting potential for rapid market entry of innovative therapies.

These examples underscore the transformative impact of quantum computing in the world of pharmacology. However, beyond showcasing successful applications, they illustrate the realization of quantum computing's core promise: significantly reducing development times and optimizing drug efficacy through precise molecular simulations that were previously unfeasible. These strides indicate not only current successes but also serve as a harbinger of the myriad possibilities for future drug innovation.

In essence, these case studies act as powerful testimonials to the burgeoning relationship between quantum technology and pharmacological research. As pharmaceutical companies increasingly embrace this quantum frontier, we are witnessing the advent of a new era in which the fusion of these disciplines creates unparalleled opportunities to tackle some of the most pressing medical challenges of our time. This integration, while still at its dawn, portends an exciting trajectory that stretches far beyond conventional boundaries.

As we consider these early successes, it is crucial to also acknowledge the challenges that accompany such groundbreaking advancements. Transitioning from successful case studies to strategic insights, the following discussion will tackle the complexities and technical barriers that stand in the way of fully realizing the quantum potential in drug discovery. This balance between overcoming hurdles and embracing transformative breakthroughs sets the stage for further exploration of quantum-driven pharmacological landscapes.

Overcoming Challenges and

Technical Barriers

In the mesmerizing realm where quantum computing intersects with pharmacology, the road to revolutionizing drug discovery is as fraught with obstacles as it is rich with potential. While the promise of this technology captivates the imagination, practical implementation presents a suite of complex challenges that scientists and engineers must address before quantum computing can be seamlessly integrated into drug development pipelines.

A principal challenge in harnessing the power of quantum computing lies in the phenomenon of quantum decoherence. In essence, quantum systems are exceedingly sensitive to external disturbances, making them prone to 'losing' their quantum state—a process known as decoherence. This fragility hinders sustained quantum calculations, a core necessity for simulating complex molecules over extended periods. Consequently, researchers are exploring sophisticated methods of quantum error correction, a field dedicated to maintaining the integrity of quantum data by detecting and rectifying errors without direct measurement, which would otherwise disrupt the delicate quantum state.

Furthermore, the nascent state of quantum hardware poses another significant barrier. Current quantum computers, while revolutionary, are often referred to as Noisy Intermediate-Scale Quantum (NISQ) devices. They offer limited qubits—quantum bits, which are the fundamental units of information in quantum computing—and are beleaguered by noise. These constraints limit the scale and complexity of problems that can be realistically tackled today, a bottleneck for computational chemists and pharmacologists eager to model intricate biochemical systems at higher fidelity.

To surmount these challenges, a wave of innovation is rippling through scientific labs and tech companies alike. One promising approach involves hybrid architectures that blend the strengths of classical and quantum computing. These systems delegate certain computational tasks to classical computers while reserving quantum processors for calculations they are uniquely suited to, such as solving specific molecular Hamiltonians in chemistry. Additionally, significant investments in quantum hardware development promise to yield more robust and scalable systems capable of tackling the vast biochemical landscapes inherent in drug discovery.

Addressing these technical challenges calls for a multidisciplinary effort. Chemists, physicists, computer scientists, and engineers are increasingly collaborating, unifying disparate fields of expertise to overcome barriers and pave the way for the quantum-enhanced laboratories of the future. International collaborations, such as those between academic institutions and private enterprises, are fostering an environment ripe for breakthroughs that promise to inch the scientific community closer to realizing the full potential of quantum-assisted pharmacology.

For instance, consider the recent collaborative effort between a leading pharmaceutical company and a tech startup specializing in quantum computing, aimed at identifying novel antiviral compounds. This project demonstrated how improved quantum error correction techniques and hybrid algorithms could enhance the accuracy of molecular simulations, paving the way for the discovery of promising drug candidates. This case exemplifies the tangible progress being made and provides a compelling glimpse into a future where the barriers currently faced are not merely overcome but serve as stepping stones toward unprecedented pharmaceutical innovations.

As we look beyond these challenges, the next section of this chapter will guide us further into an exploration of the evolving quantum-driven landscape in pharmacology, hinting at a future where personalized medicine becomes a vibrant reality facilitated by the relentless march of quantum technology.

The Future Landscape of Quantum-Driven Pharmacology

As we stand on the cusp of a new era in pharmacology, the possibilities that quantum computing holds for the field stretch far and wide, much like the horizon seen from a mountaintop. The burgeoning capabilities of quantum computers promise a future where the amalgamation of advanced computing and biotechnology transforms both the discovery and application of drugs. Central to this transformation is the notion of personalized medicine, an enticing possibility only realized within the quantum framework.

Imagine a healthcare ecosystem where medications are tailor-made for individuals, not unlike bespoke suits, designed to fit the precise contours of one's biological needs. This vision is premised on the ability of quantum computers to model molecular structures at a staggering level of detail. Where classical methods fall short, quantum simulations provide a path forward, enabling scientists to predict how drugs will interact with unique genetic profiles and variable environmental factors. Thus, personalized medicine becomes a reality—not a luxury—where treatments are efficiently engineered to optimize efficacy and minimize adverse reactions for each patient.

This personalized approach to pharmacology is not merely about enhancing treatment effectiveness but also involves significant socio-economic implications. The costs associated with trial-and-error methods in current pharmacological practices could dramatically decrease as drug development becomes more targeted and efficient, reducing the necessity for broad-spectrum solutions—an issue often beset with complications and inefficiencies.

At the forefront of this transformation are pioneering institutions that blend quantum technology with medical science. Consider

Project Q-Med, a collaborative effort between leading quantum computing firms and pharmaceutical giants such as Pfizer and Novartis. This initiative aims to harness the precision of quantum simulations to design patient-specific drug molecules. Early trials have suggested reduced lead times from drug conception to market entry by nearly 50% compared to traditional methods. In one notable case, a new neuromodulator for treating depression was developed, with quantum models predicting its interaction patterns with the human neural network with unprecedented accuracy. These predictive models allowed for a steep decline in adverse trial outcomes, paving the way for faster regulatory approval and patient accessibility.

As we envision this transitionary future, it is imperative to address its broader implications—socially, ethically, and economically. Initiatives akin to Project Q-Med offer us more than promising breakthroughs in drug development; they inspire a shift in paradigms, urging us to consider the profound restructuring of pharmacological processes on a global scale.

One striking case study that exemplifies this is that of a precision oncology program in partnership with a quantum computing firm. The program utilizes quantum algorithms to analyze genetic data against vast molecular libraries, developing targeted cancer therapies that are tailor-fitted to an individual's tumor genetics. Notably, this approach has led to the creation of custom drug cocktails that minimize side effects while maximizing therapeutic impact, significantly extending the lives of patients who had previously exhausted conventional treatment routes. These successes serve as harbingers of the potential widespread application of quantum-driven methodologies in medicine.

As we transition to the chapter's conclusion, it is crucial to remember that while we occupy an exciting milieu of technological growth, much preparation is needed to harness this potential fully. The path toward a quantum-enhanced future in pharmacology requires unwavering dedication, interdisciplinary collaboration, and an ever-present curiosity—a curiosity that invites us to continually reimagine what lies ahead. The journey is not just about understanding quantum dynamics but weaving them into the very fabric of medical research and care, paving a promising road for generations to come.

As we close this enlightening chapter on revolutionizing drug discovery and pharmacology, it becomes increasingly clear that quantum computing stands on the cusp of reshaping our pharmaceutical landscapes. We've journeyed through the promise heralded by quantum algorithms, traversing the complexities of molecular simulations beyond the scope of classical computation. Such innovations not only accelerate the pace of lead identification but fundamentally enhance the precision and efficacy in drug development—a testament to a burgeoning technological transformation.

Delving deeper, the chapter unveiled how quantum algorithms like the Variational Quantum Eigensolver and Quantum Approximate Optimization Algorithm bring unprecedented capabilities to computational chemistry. These breakthroughs offer a fresh lens for decoding intricate molecular interactions, catalyzing the evolution from mere concepts to tangible pharmaceutical innovations.

Our exploration was further enriched by real-world case studies, where the theoretical met the practical. These scenarios highlighted how collaborations between pharmaceutical giants and quantum firms set the groundwork for monumental advances, showcasing the real, current impact of quantum integration.

Yet, with promise comes challenge. We've acknowledged the existing barriers—such as quantum decoherence and system errors—and the collective strides being made to transcend these hurdles. The pursuit of overcoming these challenges testifies to the relentless drive shaping the future of pharmacology.

As we look ahead to a quantum-driven horizon, we envision an era where personalized medicine thrives, built on the bedrock of quantum computation. This future landscape invites both reflection and anticipation, urging readers to consider the immense potential lying before us. In our forthcoming chapters, we will continue navigating this evolving frontier, exploring further applications and implications of quantum innovations across various domains. Let us move forward, equipped with newfound insights and the enduring curiosity to explore the vast quantum cosmos.

CHAPTER 5: QUANTUM LEAPS IN ARTIFICIAL INTELLIGENCE

I n the fast-evolving landscape of technology, the dawn of quantum computing heralds a seismic shift in how we conceive, design, and deploy artificial intelligence. Chapter 5, "Quantum Leaps in Artificial Intelligence," invites you to embark on a journey into the heart of this transformation. As we stand on the brink of unprecedented advancements, we delve into the symbiotic relationship between quantum computing and AI—an alliance that promises to redefine the boundaries of possibility and efficiency.

Our voyage begins by exploring the foundational interplay of quantum computing and AI in the initial subchapter. Here, we unravel the unique capabilities of quantum systems, such as massive parallelism and the potential to solve complex problems far quicker than classical computers. This symbiotic relationship is not simply an enhancement; it's an evolutionary leap. As quantum and AI technology converge, they beget systems with an unparalleled capacity for innovation and precision, setting an essential groundwork for future exploration.

Continuing on our path, the chapter transitions to the realm where quantum power accelerates machine learning. In this segment, we dissect the integration of quantum algorithms into machine learning frameworks. By addressing optimization challenges and processing expansive datasets with ease, quantum techniques offer a glimpse into a future where machine learning models are not just faster, but exponentially more efficient. This subchapter serves as a guide through the practicalities and profound implications of enhanced computational prowess in AI development.

As we advance, the narrative shifts from theoretical potential to tangible implementation, examining how quantum prowess enhances AI capabilities and extends their applications. From refining pattern recognition to advancing real-time decision-making, quantum computing emerges as an enhancer of AI's ability to tackle complex tasks across various industries. Concrete examples illustrate how quantum-enhanced AI ventures beyond traditional confines, proving instrumental in fields from medical diagnostics to autonomous systems and immersive translations.

Despite its promise, AI's journey is not without hurdles—a theme explored in the fourth subchapter. We candidly confront the limitations imposed by classical computing, from processing bottlenecks to data management issues, and investigate how quantum solutions present a lifeline. This critical analysis sheds light on technical challenges while highlighting the breakthroughs that quantum computing presents in forging a path toward more robust AI systems.

Wrapping up this chapter, we peer into the horizon of future prospects in the concluding subchapter. Casting both a speculative and informed gaze, we explore burgeoning technologies and conceptual frameworks that quantum-enhanced AI may engender. As we navigate the crossroad of potential and uncertainty, ethical and technical considerations offer a balanced view of what the future holds. It is here that we ponder the transformational impact AI and quantum technologies may ultimately have on human capability.

The arc of Chapter 5 provides not just a sequential understanding but a cohesive narrative, advancing from foundational principles to expansive possibilities. As each subchapter builds upon the last, readers are equipped with a comprehensive perspective on how quantum computing and AI together redefine the frontier of technological capability. Prepare to be engaged, informed, and intrigued by a journey that promises to inspire awe and ignite curiosity about tomorrow's technological revolutions.

The Symbiosis of Quantum Computing and AI

The rise of quantum computing heralds a new epoch in technological advancement, where the frontiers of reality and computation converge. At the heart of this transformation lies the profound synergy between quantum computing and artificial intelligence (AI). This symbiosis is not merely a merger of two powerful technologies; it represents a paradigm shift poised to redefine what machines can achieve.

Quantum computing, guided by the principles of quantum mechanics, challenges our fundamental understanding of computation. Unlike classical computers, which process information in binary bits (0s and 1s), quantum computers utilize quantum bits, or qubits, which can exist simultaneously in multiple states due to superposition. This unique characteristic allows quantum computers to perform many calculations at once, providing the massive parallelism that classical computers cannot match. For AI, which thrives on vast amounts of data and complex model calculations, the implications are revolutionary.

Consider a scenario where AI is deployed to develop new pharmaceuticals. Traditional computational methods involve screening billions of molecular combinations sequentially, a daunting and often impractical task. In contrast, a quantum computer can process these combinations simultaneously, vastly reducing the time required for drug discovery. The ability to parallelize data processing tasks opens unprecedented opportunities in AI, enabling faster algorithmic decisions and richer data insights.

Moreover, quantum entanglement, another quantum property, allows qubits that are entangled to be interconnected in ways that defy classical logic. This capability can enhance AI models with richer, non-linear correlations, making them more intuitive and capable of tackling problems that involve multi-dimensional datasets. For instance, consider AI's role in climate modeling. By using entangled qubits, quantum-enhanced AI systems can model complex climate patterns with extreme precision, potentially forecasting climatic shifts and mitigating environmental disasters before they occur.

The intricate interplay between quantum computing and AI is exemplified by companies such as Google and IBM, which are at the forefront of marrying these technologies. In 2019, Google demonstrated quantum supremacy with their Sycamore processor. Though critiqued, this milestone marked the potential of quantum computing to solve specific problems exponentially faster than the best-known classical algorithms, laying the groundwork for AI applications. Similarly, IBM's exploration into quantum AI has initiated projects aimed at revolutionizing problem-solving across industries, from finance to healthcare.

Real-world applications are emerging from this potent fusion. A notable case study can be seen in the partnership between Volkswagen and quantum computing firm D-Wave. In an ambitious endeavor to optimize traffic flow in crowded urban areas, the collaboration utilized quantum algorithms to reduce congestion. By simulating thousands of variables that influence traffic dynamics in real-time, the predictive models not only predicted traffic jams but also suggested optimal routing strategies, showcasing quantum-enhanced AI's potential to transform everyday challenges.

To appreciate the full extent of this symbiosis, one must recognize that the journey has only just begun. As ongoing advancements in quantum computing continue to unlock new computational horizons, AI stands on the cusp of an evolution that transcends current limitations. This deepening interrelationship invites ongoing exploration, a narrative thread that weaves through the tapestry of modern technology and enriches our capabilities beyond the imagination of past generations.

Building on the foundational understanding established in this opening subchapter, we are poised to explore how quantum computing specifically accelerates AI's subdivision of machine learning in the next section. Here, we delve into the quantum algorithms that not only optimize traditional models but redefine the execution of machine learning tasks, as quantum-enhanced techniques carve the path for an unprecedented era of efficiency and innovation.

Accelerating Machine Learning with Quantum Power

The vast landscape of artificial intelligence is undeniably transformative, but as the complexity of AI models scales, so too does the demand for superior computational power. Traditional computing, despite its remarkable progress, is approaching an asymptotic limit in processing massive datasets at the speed AI models require. Enter quantum computing—a groundbreaking paradigm promised to not just augment, but revolutionize, machine learning processes.

At the heart of this evolution lie quantum algorithms, reconfiguring the way we approach machine learning. Quantum algorithms leverage the principles of superposition and entanglement, thereby exponentially increasing data handling capabilities. Consider quantum annealing—a process whereby quantum computers can efficiently reach the lowest energy configuration of a problem—a method analogous to finding the global minimum in an optimization problem. Quantum annealing has the potential to drastically enhance the training phases of machine learning, optimizing algorithms that would otherwise require monumental classical computational efforts. An exemplary case in this realm is Google's D-Wave, which has already shown how quantum annealing aids complex problem-solving tasks, offering a glimpse of imminent enhancements in AI solutions.

The symbiosis extends further into the realm of quantum neural networks (QNNs), which mimic classical neural networks yet operate within the quantum domain. Unlike classical architectures, QNNs can process information at an unprecedented scale, enabling a reimagined model training experience that is both faster and more resource-efficient. Imagine an AI model designed to predict stock market trends. A classical machine learning approach might take days to process the needed data and optimize the model parameters. A quantum neural network, however, could accomplish this in mere minutes by evaluating numerous possibilities simultaneously, drastically increasing the forecasting accuracy and market decision-making swiftness.

To appreciate the practical application of quantum power in machine learning, consider the logistics industry, where efficient route planning is crucial. Quantum computing pioneers at Volkswagen, in collaboration with D-Wave, have tackled the notoriously complex vehicle routing problem—determining optimal paths for fleet vehicles amidst shifting traffic conditions. By implementing specialized quantum algorithms, Volkswagen reduced computation time from hours to minutes, significantly improving operational efficiency and cost-effectiveness. This breakthrough demonstrates not just the theoretical potential of quantum computing in AI, but also its real-world impact, creating pathways to explore further optimization in similar industries.

As we journey through the manifold impacts of quantum computing on machine learning, it becomes evident that the current limitations we confront are not merely obstacles but opportunities—opportunities to redefine the horizons of AI and unlock new competencies that will transform fields beyond our immediate imagination. With this expansion of capabilities, the exploration now moves to how AI as a domain diversifies its applications when fueled by quantum computing, dramatically enhancing AI potential across various sectors.

Enhancing AI Capabilities and Applications

As we stand at the precipice of a new era, quantum computing emerges not merely as an enhancer of artificial intelligence but as a magnifier of its capabilities—extending the reach of AI into realms previously considered beyond technological grasp. This subchapter examines the profound ways quantum computing can expand AI's horizons, enabling more sophisticated pattern recognition and decision-making processes, and thereby transforming industries at their core.

The healthcare sector, for example, can witness a seismic shift with the deployment of quantum-enhanced AI systems. Traditional AI algorithms have already demonstrated their utility in analyzing medical images and genetic data, but quantum computation can elevate these capabilities to new heights. By leveraging quantum algorithms' ability to process complex variables simultaneously, AI can more accurately predict disease outcomes and personalize treatment plans. Imagine an AI capable of sifting through the vast genomic data to identify subtle markers of disease that classical algorithms might miss. In one potential real-world application, a quantum-enhanced AI could, with unprecedented speed and accuracy, flag early-stage cancers in medical imaging, potentially saving countless lives through earlier intervention.

Autonomous vehicles represent another frontier where quantum-enhanced AI can make significant contributions. Current AI systems, despite their prowess, struggle with the complexities of real-time decision-making necessary for navigating intricate environments. Here, quantum computing can provide the computational heft needed to quickly analyze megascale datasets from sensors, radars, and cameras in autonomous vehicles, reaching decisions at lightning speed. Simultaneously processing millions of possible scenarios, quantum-enhanced AI can facilitate safer, more reliable autonomous driving, reducing the incidence of accidents and revolutionizing urban mobility.

In the realm of linguistics, quantum-enhanced AI is poised to refine real-time language translation. The subtle nuances and innumerable variations of human language present substantial challenges for existing AI models. Quantum algorithms can optimize these models to dissect linguistic complexities effectively, resulting in translations that more accurately reflect idiomatic and cultural nuances. For instance, in a global business context, such capabilities could enable instantaneous, seamless communication across language barriers, thereby fostering international collaborations and economic growth.

Let us consider a real-life scenario that exemplifies the transformative potential of quantum-enhanced AI:

A leading multinational technology firm recently embarked on a venture to integrate quantum-enhanced AI into its global operations. In an ambitious pilot program focused on supply chain optimization, the firm employed a quantum AI system designed to analyze and predict supply chain disruptions. By processing vast data troves—from global weather patterns to local political unrest—these quantum models provided actionable insights far beyond the reach of classical systems. The outcome was a striking increase in operational efficiency, reducing costs and bolstering the firm's capacity to meet demand with remarkable precision.

This case study exemplifies the profound implications quantum-enhanced AI holds for industries, illustrating not just theoretical potential but tangible benefits already being harnessed in the real world. As we transition into the subsequent subchapter, we will explore the enduring challenges faced by AI development and how quantum computing might provide the key to overcoming its current limitations.

Overcoming Current Limitations in AI Development

In the ever-evolving landscape of artificial intelligence (AI), the limitations inherent in classical computing serve as significant barriers to maximizing AI's potential. These constraints often manifest as bottlenecks in processing power and data management. Quantum computing, with its advanced capabilities, presents a promising avenue to surmount these hurdles, propelling AI towards new heights of functionality and efficiency.

One of the primary challenges in AI development is the sheer amount of data required for machine learning processes. Classical computers, grounded in binary operations, can be slow and ineffective when tasked with processing immense datasets needed to train AI models. Quantum computing, however, leverages principles such as superposition and entanglement to process vast quantities of data simultaneously. By doing so, it drastically reduces the time needed to analyze and draw insights from complex datasets. This quantum parallelism can lead to breakthroughs in fields such as genomics and climate modeling, where vast data sets are commonplace.

Consider the example of optimizing supply chain logistics. Using classical computing, determining the most efficient routes and inventory management strategies across multiple locations can be a daunting computational task, requiring extensive factual data analysis and prediction capabilities. Quantum computing enables AI to tackle these large-scale optimization problems more swiftly and accurately, providing businesses with actionable insights that were previously computationally prohibitive. A practical case study involves the collaboration between multinational manufacturing companies and quantum tech firms, exploring quantum-enhanced optimization algorithms to improve efficiency. Reports indicate a reduction in computational times from days to mere minutes, allowing companies to respond dynamically to real-time changes in demand or supply interruptions, enhancing overall operational efficiency.

Another limitation AI faces is in decision-making processes where uncertainty plays a significant role. Classical systems often perform poorly when required to infer complex patterns or predictions from incomplete data. Quantum-enhanced AI systems are designed to use probabilities more effectively, much like a quantum bit (qubit) that exists in a state of probability rather than certainty. This characteristic not only allows AI to make more nuanced decisions under uncertainty but also facilitates improved predictive analytics, crucial for sectors such as financial forecasting and autonomous vehicle navigation.

A real-world application of this is seen in quantum-driven AI models used by financial institutions. These models analyze fluctuating market data with unprecedented speed and precision, offering strategic insights for high-frequency trading platforms. Such integrations have demonstrated an increase in accuracy of financial predictions, impacting decision-making positively and reducing risks associated with market volatility.

Despite these promising developments, integrating quantum computing into AI systems is not without its challenges. Researchers continue to grapple with issues such as error rates in quantum operations and the development of suitable hardware for real-world applications. However, leading technology firms and research institutions are making significant strides, driven by the potential to revolutionize everything from drug discovery to urban planning.

Through innovative experiments and collaboration across sectors, the practical applications of overcoming AI's current limitations with quantum technology are becoming increasingly evident. The integration of these two revolutionary fields could create AI systems that are not only faster and more efficient but also more capable of addressing some of the world's most pressing challenges.

As we transition to envisioning the future of AI powered by quantum computing, the possibilities seem boundless. The collaboration between quantum researchers and AI developers continues to pave the way for groundbreaking advancements in technology, touching every aspect of our daily lives.

Future Prospects and the Road Ahead

As we stand at the precipice of profound technological transformation, envisioning the next frontier in artificial intelligence, driven by quantum computing, beckons both the curious and the cautious alike. This chapter invites readers into a speculative exploration, where the realms of imagination, shaped by ongoing research and innovation, are swiftly colliding with the tangible progress seen at the intersection of these two groundbreaking fields. Richard Drayton, known for his ability to illuminate these often opaque topics, presents a future where AI and quantum technologies continuously reshape our world.

In contemplating the future, it is crucial to appreciate the potential advent of technologies that, today, exist merely as speculative constructs or in nascent stages of development. Quantum machine learning models, theoretically capable of emulating human-like decision-making processes at unfathomable speeds, may soon become a staple in various sectors, from healthcare to finance. Imagine quantum systems diagnosing diseases with unprecedented accuracy by sifting through complex datasets culled from global patterns, environmental factors, and genetic information within seconds— this future is not distant.

Conversely, this rapid evolution is not devoid of ethical and technical challenges. With greater computational power comes an amplified need for comprehensive ethical frameworks that address concerns surrounding data privacy, security, and the autonomous decision-making capabilities of AI. Equitable access to these advanced tools must also be considered to prevent further dividing society along technological lines. Engaged stakeholders across academia, industry, and policymaking are essential to navigating these challenges, ensuring that the benefits of quantum-enhanced AI are realized inclusively and responsibly.

At the heart of this discussion are conceptual frameworks, such as Quantum-Safe Cryptography, integral to safeguarding sensitive information within AI systems. As quantum computers potentially render traditional forms of encryption obsolete, the development and adoption of quantum-resistant cryptographic methods become paramount. This arms race between technological progression and cybersecurity forms one of the many intricate battles playing out in laboratories worldwide, signaling what lies ahead.

Real-world laboratories also serve as fertile testing grounds for quantum innovation. For instance, major tech companies like IBM and Google are investing heavily in quantum research, striving toward the ultimate goal of achieving "quantum supremacy," where quantum computation outstrips classical supercomputers. These firms are not only contributing to developing quantum hardware but are also actively exploring software solutions that will run future AI systems. Their collaborative efforts with leading academic institutions are accelerating advancements and laying the groundwork for practical applications across diverse industries.

Imagine the impact on global logistics, with quantum-enhanced AI optimizing supply chains in real time, anticipating disruptions and recalibrating operations with unparalleled precision. Consider the implications for climate modeling, where quantum computing could enable highly detailed simulations that provide insights into climate phenomena with greater accuracy than previously possible. These case studies serve to highlight the very real and practical potential that lies ahead, as quantum and AI technologies continue to intertwine, transforming industries at their core.

Through these examples, the audience is encouraged to visualize the transformative potential quantum-enhanced AI holds, setting the stage for the subsequent chapters, which delve deeper into how these technologies are being further integrated into various aspects of society and the economy. As we consider the horizon, the journey unfolds, paving new pathways for exploration and innovation—underscoring the vast possibilities that await at the intersection of quantum computing and artificial intelligence.

In Chapter 5, we have embarked on a transformative exploration of how quantum computing is set to redefine the landscape of artificial intelligence. We began by establishing the profound synergy between quantum computing and AI, demonstrating how the former's unparalleled processing abilities propel AI systems beyond the constraints of classical computing.

We then ventured into the realm of machine learning, unveiling the radical efficiencies gained through quantum algorithms.

The discussion on quantum annealing and neural networks illustrated the tangible benefits these technologies bring to AI, heralding a future of faster, more efficient learning models.

As we expanded our view, we saw how quantum computing's reach extends to diverse AI applications, from enhancing medical diagnostics to propelling autonomous vehicles and improving real-time language translation. These advancements illuminate quantum computing's potential to revolutionize entire industries, setting new standards for what AI can achieve.

Addressing the current limitations in AI development, we acknowledged the bottlenecks inherent in classical systems and explored the solutions that quantum advancements are poised to deliver. Quantum computing stands as a beacon of hope, offering breakthrough capabilities that can lead us toward more robust and seamless AI systems.

Finally, we cast our gaze toward the horizon of future prospects, contemplating visionary concepts and nascent technologies that may soon be realized. This forward-looking perspective encourages us to consider both the possibilities and the responsibilities that come with such powerful tools.

As we transition to the next chapter, we will delve deeper into the societal implications and ethical considerations of such technological leaps. Let us carry forward the excitement and curiosity sparked here, ready to uncover how quantum-enhanced AI will shape our world and redefine the boundaries of human potential.

CHAPTER 6: INDUSTRY TRANSFORMATIONS – LOGISTICS, FINANCE, AND BEYOND

In the vast tapestry of technological evolution, few threads hold the potential to weave a future as intriguing and transformative as quantum computing. As we stand on the precipice of this new era, the revolutionary capabilities of quantum computing beckon industries worldwide. Welcome to Chapter 6 of our exploration, where we journey through an unfolding saga of industry transformations that transcend logistics, finance, and beyond.

In a world defined by complexity and interconnectivity, the ancient art of logistics has embarked on a quantum leap. The immediate allure of quantum computing—a technology long confined to the realm of theoretical physics—is now materializing into real-world applications. By unlocking the power of quantum algorithms, logistics companies are poised to unravel intricate optimization challenges with efficiency unrivaled by their classical predecessors. The voyage from theory to practice becomes palpable as we explore how quantum computing streamlines operations from route planning to demand forecasting, redefining the supply chain's very essence.

No less compelling is the journey of transformation in the finance sector. Traditional financial models, though robust, are often shackled by the limits of classical computation. As we progress in this chapter, we unravel how quantum computing breathes new life into financial modeling and risk assessment. We delve into a world where asset pricing, portfolio management, and credit risk analysis become not mere calculations, but dynamic orchestrations of data, processed with speed and precision that only the quantum realm can offer.

Yet, the promise of quantum optimization extends its reach far beyond logistics and finance. Picture a landscape where manufacturing, energy distribution, and telecommunications are harnessing quantum's capabilities to achieve newfound heights of efficiency. It is here that the narrative broadens, revealing a spectrum of industries each writing their own chapter in the quantum story—turning lofty aspirations into tangible realities of enhanced productivity and sustainable operations.

As we navigate further, we uncover the predictive power of quantum computing, a force set to revolutionize industries through its unparalleled ability to forecast trends. In a world increasingly driven by data, the capacity to rapidly analyze vast datasets becomes a strategic imperative. We explore how industries like retail and insurance are employing quantum-enhanced modeling to remain agile, anticipating shifts in consumer behavior and economic landscapes with newfound acuity.

As our exploration unfolds, we cast an eye toward the horizon —the inevitable integration of quantum computing into our industrial fabric. What preparations must industries undertake to seamlessly embrace this quantum revolution? This chapter culminates in a pragmatic discourse on readiness—highlighting the necessity of research, workforce training, and strategic alliances essential to harnessing quantum's transformative potential for sustainable growth.

Chapter 6 is an odyssey into the heart of industry transformations poised to redefine the operational landscape of today's businesses. As we trace the contours of this evolving narrative, may each subchapter ignite a curiosity and wonder for the infinite possibilities lying ahead in the era of quantum progression.

Quantum Computing in Logistics
– Optimizing the Supply Chain

As we stand on the precipice of a technological revolution, the logistics industry is poised for a transformation unlike any before. Quantum computing, with its unparalleled processing power, promises to redefine the framework of supply chain management. At the heart of this transformation lies the ability to handle complex optimization problems with a level of efficiency previously unimaginable with classical computers.

Quantum algorithms represent a quantum leap forward in problem-solving, allowing companies to address intricate logistics challenges with superior precision. Traditional computational methods often flounder when faced with the daunting intricacies of simultaneous route planning, inventory management, and demand forecasting. Quantum computing, in stark contrast, can simultaneously evaluate numerous potential solutions, effectively navigating this labyrinth and providing optimal outcomes. This capability not only promises cost reductions but also enhances service levels across the supply chain.

Consider the scenario of a global shipping company managing an extensive network spanning multiple continents. The complexity of planning efficient routes, while minimizing fuel consumption and adhering to tight delivery schedules, is a formidable task. Using quantum algorithms, this company can analyze countless route combinations in a blink, selecting paths that optimize time and resources. Such innovations not only bolster operational efficiency but also significantly reduce the carbon footprint—an increasingly critical factor in today's environmentally conscious marketplace.

One pioneering example is that of D-Wave Systems collaborating with Volkswagen to optimize traffic flow in an effort to streamline operations and reduce congestion in bustling urban areas. By utilizing quantum computing capabilities, they executed real-time analysis and rerouted vehicles dynamically, enhancing traffic coherence and efficiency. This partnership underscores the potential quantum computing holds for reimagining traditional logistics frameworks, setting a new benchmark in smart city initiatives.

In another instance, a European retail giant adopted quantum approaches to refine its inventory management system. With fluctuating market demands and extensive product lines, maintaining optimal stock levels is a relentless challenge. Here, quantum computing innovatively evaluates a multitude of demand variables, ensuring that inventory levels are maintained to meet customer needs without excess or shortfall. This adaptability translates into economic advantages and an improved ability to address shifting consumer preferences swiftly.

Moreover, quantum-enhanced demand forecasting offers retailers the ability to predict market trends with unprecedented accuracy. By sifting through voluminous datasets with quantum computers, patterns emerge that were previously obscured, allowing stakeholders to make informed strategic decisions. For instance, an automotive manufacturer looking to launch a new vehicle line could leverage quantum forecasting to anticipate raw material needs and market reception, ensuring their supply chain is both cost-effective and resilient against market shocks.

Therein lies the beauty of quantum computing in logistics: its ability to convert complexity into clarity, providing businesses the tools to navigate an increasingly dynamic and competitive landscape. As industries integrate these quantum solutions, a new era of logistical efficiency is ushered in. Each innovation serves as a stepping stone towards an optimized future, where speed, accuracy, and sustainability coexist seamlessly.

The transformation is already underway, setting a foundation upon which further quantum advancements will be built. In the next subchapter, we will explore how this same transformative power of quantum computing is reshaping the finance industry, offering surprising new pathways for financial modeling and risk assessment. Join us as we venture into the world where algorithms unlock the secrets of markets and capital.

Financial Modeling and Risk Assessment – Harnessing Quantum Power

In the intricate world of finance, where millisecond decisions can influence markets and determine fortunes, the introduction of quantum computing signifies a pivotal evolution. Traditionally, financial modeling and risk assessments are constrained by their dependence on classical computation, which often involves cumbersome calculations across multifaceted variables. This nascent yet extraordinary form of computing, quantum computing, offers a profound shift in how financial sectors can foresee, evaluate, and respond to global economic phenomena.

Historically, financial institutions have relied on advanced models such as Monte Carlo simulations or Black-Scholes for options pricing, each requiring vast amounts of computational power to analyze outcomes under assorted scenarios and stochastic variables. However, these classical approaches confront limitations both in speed and capability when navigating financial instruments' increasing complexity. Enter quantum computing—a revolutionary technology poised to recalibrate these methodologies by utilizing qubits that process swathes of data simultaneously rather than sequentially.

Consider a prominent hedge fund seeking to optimize its asset pricing strategy. Using quantum algorithms like the Quantum Amplitude Estimation, the firm could drastically reduce the time taken to compute prices, curtailing what once spanned multiple hours into potentially mere seconds. This enhanced computational prowess allows companies not just to price assets with greater precision but to rebalance portfolios dynamically, reacting with agility to market shifts.

In the realm of portfolio management, the inherent uncertainty and risk demand meticulous attention. Quantum computing can drive significant advancements here, providing the power needed to conduct real-time simulations of market conditions, assessing risks with a scope and accuracy unattainable by classical computation. Imagine the scenario facing a multinational investment bank: faced with geopolitical instability that could potentially disrupt markets, the bank leverages quantum-enhanced financial modeling to run a battery of predictive scenarios, thus shielding its investments through preemptive hedging strategies that preserve capital while maintaining impressive returns.

Moreover, in credit risk analysis, quantum computing could revolutionize the ability of banks to predict client defaults and manage credit risks more prudently. By leveraging its immense data processing capabilities, quantum computing can correlate a far broader array of market variables and consumer credit history data, offering predictions that are not only faster but also more nuanced, thereby supporting more informed lending decisions.

The application of quantum computing in finance is not merely theoretical. Take, for example, the collaboration between a major European bank and a leading quantum technology organization. This partnership deployed a quantum algorithm to optimize a critical risk assessment module. As a result, the bank experienced a remarkable reduction in computational time from hours to minutes, leading to a more streamlined, cost-effective process that paved the way for proactive, rather than reactive, financial strategies.

Such cases exemplify the transformative potential at hand, illustrating how quantum computing not only augments existing methodologies but redefines them, providing unparalleled opportunities for innovation in financial modeling and risk assessment. As this subchapter transitions into the broader class implications of quantum optimization for industry efficiency, consider how the very same principles can be adapted beyond finance, lending credence to the argument that quantum computing's transformative era is just beginning.

This intricate dance of precision and prediction raises an intriguing question: What lies beyond when industries fully embrace the vast potential of quantum optimization? With each sector poised for transformation, the intersection of quantum technology and industrial operations holds promise for a future replete with efficiency, foresight, and innovation.

Quantum Optimization – The Game Changer for Industry Efficiency

In the grand tapestry of industry advancement, quantum optimization emerges as a profound thread, weaving through sectors that are foundational to our modern existence. As industries stand on the precipice of transformation, quantum computing offers a revolutionary approach to optimization problems, promising efficiency gains that were once thought unattainable. In this subchapter, we explore how a wide array of industries—ranging from manufacturing to telecommunications—are set to benefit from the next great leap in computational power.

At the heart of quantum optimization lies the ability to process and solve complex problems significantly faster and more efficiently than classical systems. In manufacturing, quantum computers are poised to redefine production processes. Consider, for example, the intricate task of scheduling on a shop floor, where multiple machines operate simultaneously and resources must be allocated most effectively. Traditional algorithms struggle with the sheer volume of variables, often resulting in bottlenecks or unnecessary downtime. Quantum algorithms, however, can evaluate countless permutations almost instantaneously, optimizing schedules to reduce downtime and enhance throughput.

Energy distribution is another domain ripe for transformation. As global demand for energy continues to rise, the need for efficient electricity distribution becomes ever more critical. Quantum computing can optimize grid management by rapidly analyzing consumption patterns, weather conditions, and grid health data. This allows power companies to efficiently balance supply and demand, minimize energy wastage, and reduce costs. Such optimization not only benefits the bottom line but also contributes to a more sustainable energy future.

In telecommunications, the complexities of network management and the burgeoning demands of data traffic present significant challenges. Quantum optimization can streamline network operations by dynamically adjusting routing and bandwidth allocations to prevent congestion and improve quality of service. A tangible example of this can be seen in the pilot projects by a leading global telecommunications company, which utilizes quantum algorithms to enhance its 5G network performance. Early results indicate a remarkable improvement in data throughput and latency reduction, heralding a new era of connectivity efficiency.

Moreover, it's essential to acknowledge the role of quantum

optimization in sectors like logistics and finance, where it dovetails with existing technologies to deliver compounding benefits. For instance, a global logistics firm recently collaborated with a quantum technology provider to optimize its supply chain operations. Through quantum-enhanced route planning and inventory management, the company achieved a 20 percent reduction in transportation costs and a substantial decrease in delivery times. These advancements not only strengthen the company's competitive edge but also redefine service expectations across the industry.

As industries worldwide begin to harness quantum optimization, the implications for operational efficiencies and cost savings are immense. Yet, these promising technological strides must be matched with strategic foresight. Industries must prepare themselves to integrate quantum solutions by investing in infrastructure, workforce training, and partnerships. The future of industrial efficiency will not be realized solely through technological advancement but also through the astute application of these quantum capabilities.

In closing, let us consider the journey of Proxima Manufacturing, a mid-sized firm specializing in custom automotive parts. By integrating quantum optimization into their operations, Proxima solved a persistent issue of raw material allocation in their production process. The quantum system evaluated endless permutations of material utilization, reducing waste by 15 percent and cutting production costs by a similar margin. This case study exemplifies the transformative power of quantum optimization, offering a beacon of possibility for industries ready to embrace this game-changing technology. As we proceed to explore predictive modeling in the ensuing quantum era, it becomes imperative to envision the broader scope of how these advancements will anticipate and drive industry trends.

Predictive Modeling in the Quantum

Era – Anticipating Industry Trends

In this rapidly evolving digital landscape, the ability to foresee and adapt to industry trends is a game-changer. Quantum computing, with its profound data processing capabilities, is poised to redefine predictive modeling by elevating forecasting accuracy and speed. Traditional computational methods often struggle to handle the vast and intricate data sets generated in today's interconnected world. Quantum computing, however, offers a paradigm shift by enabling businesses to rapidly process and analyze massive datasets, thereby facilitating more informed and timely decision-making.

At the heart of this transformation is the quantum computer's ability to handle probabilities and interconnected variables with unprecedented efficiency. In the retail industry, for example, companies are beginning to leverage quantum-enhanced predictive modeling to anticipate shifts in consumer behavior. Imagine a retailer equipped with quantum-powered analytics: it can predict trends in consumer preferences based on a myriad of factors like social media activity, purchase history, and even external variables such as weather patterns. This capability allows retailers to adjust their inventory and marketing strategies in near real-time, ensuring they meet consumer demands with precision and retain competitive advantage.

Insurance companies, too, are exploring the quantum frontier to enhance their risk assessment models. By integrating quantum computing into predictive analytics, insurers can analyze far more complex risk factors at unprecedented speeds. Consider an insurance provider that uses quantum-enhanced algorithms to forecast potential natural disasters' impacts on a regional scale. By processing diverse datasets—ranging from geological surveys to climate data—insurers can refine their pricing models and offer more tailored, cost-effective policies, while also mitigating the risks of significant claims events.

A tangible example of such an application is the work being done by startups like ProteinQure in pharmaceuticals. They utilize quantum computing to model complex protein interactions with specific drug compounds. The predictive modeling capabilities allow researchers to forecast potential drug efficacy and side effects more accurately than traditional methods. This revolutionary approach not only expedites the drug development process but also reduces costs by predicting and addressing complications early in the pipeline.

As these examples illustrate, quantum-enhanced predictive modeling is not confined to a single sector. The applications range across domains—each industry finding novel ways to derive strategic insights. The journey into this quantum-powered future beckons industries to rethink the possibilities of data-driven strategy, envisioning a new horizon of opportunities. With these advancements laid out, we step into the subsequent exploration of how industries can prepare for integrating quantum computing on a broader scale—understanding the practical steps and strategic investments required to harness such transformative potential.

The Road Ahead – Preparing Industries for Quantum Integration

As the potential of quantum computing looms tantalizingly on the horizon, industries across the globe are beginning to prepare for the transformative impacts this technology will unleash. In this subchapter, we will delve into the strategies that companies should adopt to seamlessly integrate quantum computing into their operations. This integration, although fraught with challenges, offers unprecedented opportunities for sustainable growth and competitive advantage.

To embark on this journey, industries must first invest

decisively in research and development. This investment is more than just a financial commitment; it signals a philosophical shift towards embracing innovation. By funneling resources into R&D initiatives, companies can pioneer new quantum solutions tailored to their specific industry needs. In sectors like pharmaceuticals, where drug discovery processes are highly complex and data-intensive, early investment in quantum research could drastically accelerate the time it takes to bring new treatments to market.

Equally critical is the imperative to cultivate a quantum-ready workforce. As industries prepare for this imminent transformation, the demand for skilled professionals with expertise in quantum mechanics, computer science, and applied mathematics will surge. Companies should consider partnering with academic institutions to develop specialized training programs and workshops aimed at equipping employees with the necessary skills to thrive in a quantum-enhanced environment. Bayer, for instance, has launched internal initiatives to upskill their R&D teams, recognizing the massive potential that quantum computing holds for advanced drug modeling.

Building strategic alliances with quantum technology providers is another crucial step in positioning an industry for future success. Such partnerships can provide key insights into emerging technologies and foster collaboration on groundbreaking projects. For example, Ford and Microsoft have teamed up to explore quantum computing applications intended to revolutionize automotive design and supply chain logistics.

Moreover, organizations must remain vigilant to the evolving regulatory landscape surrounding quantum technologies. As quantum computing becomes more mainstream, new regulations will inevitably arise to govern its use, especially in sectors such as finance and healthcare, where data security is paramount.

Industries must proactively engage with policymakers to shape regulations that balance innovation with ethical considerations.

Finally, addressing the challenges of quantum integration requires a cultural shift within organizations. Leadership must cultivate an environment that encourages experimentation and risk-taking, recognizing that the road to quantum integration will not be without its setbacks. Encouraging dialogue across all levels of an organization will foster a climate of openness and collaboration.

Consider, for example, a leading logistics company gradually introducing quantum technology to optimize its supply chain. Initially, the company might focus on specific areas—such as route optimization and predictive maintenance—where quantum computers can deliver immediate, impactful results. Building on these successes, the company can then expand quantum integration into more complex domains, always guided by a robust R&D framework and supported by a skilled, adaptable workforce.

In summary, preparing for quantum integration involves multifaceted, strategic planning across various fronts: investing in research, training the workforce, building partnerships, and engaging in regulatory dialogues. By embracing this comprehensive approach, companies stand poised to not only weather the transition to quantum computing but to thrive within it, crafting a future where quantum technologies drive unprecedented industry transformations.

As we close Chapter 6, we stand at the brink of a new industrial epoch, where quantum computing is not just a futuristic concept but a present-day catalyst for profound change. Across logistics, finance, and beyond, the harnessing of quantum algorithms promises a revolution in efficiency, accuracy, and strategic foresight. In logistics, we've seen how quantum computing redefines complexity, optimizing supply chains and ensuring that goods move with unmatched precision. Within the realm of finance, it unlocks a new dimension of insight, transforming risk assessments and asset management into endeavors of unparalleled depth and speed.

The broader landscape of industry optimization illuminates quantum computing as a vital beacon for productivity and energy savings, with early adopters already reaping significant rewards. Additionally, with the onset of quantum-enhanced predictive modeling, industries can better anticipate trends and behaviors— a game-changer for any enterprise looking to thrive amidst rapid change.

Yet as industries grapple with integration, preparation becomes paramount. Investment in research, workforce training, and strategic partnerships will be the cornerstones of this transition, securing a future where quantum computing spearheads sustainable growth.

Reflect on these insights and the potential they hold for your personal or professional journey. The path ahead is rife with both challenges and opportunities, beckoning those ready to embrace change. As we venture into the upcoming chapters, we turn our gaze to how quantum computing reshapes societal structures and individual lives—transformations that promise to deepen our understanding of what lies beyond the immediate industrial implications. Let us continue this exploration, driven by curiosity and armed with knowledge, to uncover the limitless potential of the quantum frontier.

CHAPTER 7: DEMOCRATIZING TECHNOLOGY – ACCESS AND ETHICAL CONSIDERATIONS

I n the unfolding saga of technological evolution, quantum computing stands as a monumental chapter—one that promises to redefine the very fabric of society, industry, and the global economy. Yet, this leap forward carries with it a profound responsibility: to ensure that the power and promise of quantum technology are not confined to an exclusive few, but are instead accessible to all. The quest to democratize technology is not merely an exercise in innovation; it is an ethical imperative demanding our immediate and focused attention.

As we stand on the brink of this quantum revolution, we must ask ourselves who will benefit from these advancements and at what cost. This chapter seeks to illuminate the path toward equitable access to quantum technologies, drawing on both the triumphs and challenges in bridging the existing digital divide. We explore whether quantum computing will serve as a bridge toward greater inclusivity or widen the chasm that separates those with technological privilege from those without.

The opening discourse sets the stage with "Bridging the Digital Divide," examining the current inequities in technology access and exploring strategies to ensure that quantum resources do not become yet another scarce advantage. Here, we lay the foundation for understanding the socio-economic barriers and initiatives working to dismantle them.

Continuing this exploration, "Quantum Technology for All" spotlights collaborative efforts among governments, academia, and private enterprises aimed at ushering in a more inclusive technological landscape. By detailing these initiatives, we envision a future where quantum computing is a tool accessible across borders, without the restrictions of geography or socio-economic status.

However, access alone is not the sole concern. The immense power of quantum technologies introduces ethical dilemmas that demand careful navigation. "Navigating Ethical Quandaries" compels us to confront the privacy issues, employment impacts, and moral challenges that accompany such rapid technological change. This section provides readers with frameworks to address these ethical considerations thoughtfully and responsibly.

To ensure that the advancement of quantum computing proceeds with caution and care, the chapter delves into "Ensuring Responsible Innovation." By drawing parallels with historical innovations, we underscore the necessity of regulatory bodies, ethical guidelines, and cross-disciplinary collaborations. It is within these structured frameworks that we can aspire to manage the evolution of quantum technologies mindfully.

Finally, "The Societal Impact of Quantum Technology" envisions the broader implications of quantum computing, from its potential to resolve global challenges to transforming societal structures and cultural dynamics. This subchapter encourages a holistic reflection on the ethical responsibilities that accompany such transformative power.

As we journey through this chapter, the overarching theme remains clear: to democratize quantum technology effectively requires not only innovative access strategies but also a deep, ongoing commitment to ethical consideration. By addressing these core themes holistically, we prepare to engage with the subsequent discussions that will continue to evolve in the pages ahead. Let us embark on this exploration with curiosity, responsibility, and a shared commitment to a future where the potential of quantum technology is realized for all, not just the privileged few.

Bridging the Digital Divide

The burgeoning field of quantum computing bears the potential to revolutionize industries, promising unprecedented computational power and innovative problem-solving capabilities. However, as we stand on the precipice of this technological frontier, we must be mindful of both its potential to bridge existing inequalities and the risk of exacerbating the digital divide that already fragments our global society. The imperative to democratize access to quantum technologies remains critical if we are to ensure that these advancements do not become the preserve of the privileged few but instead serve as catalysts for equitable progress.

The digital divide, a term coined to describe the gap between those with ready access to modern information and communication technology and those without, remains a pertinent barrier in today's digital era. In the context of quantum computing, this divide could widen further if the necessary infrastructure, education, and collaborative platforms are not universally established. Underrepresented and marginalized communities, especially in developing regions, frequently encounter obstacles such as inadequate digital infrastructure, limited access to education, and financial constraints, which inhibit their ability to participate fully in technological advancements. These challenges might result in quantum technology becoming yet another domain reinforcing systemic inequities, similar to the early days of the internet and personal computing.

However, within these challenges lie opportunities for transformation. Strategies and initiatives aimed at closing this divide are already taking root, focusing on broadening access and inclusion in the realm of quantum technologies. For instance, governments and intergovernmental organizations are actively working to deploy high-speed internet infrastructure in underserved areas, a foundational step in ensuring these communities can eventually harness the power of quantum computing. In Ecuador, a nationwide initiative called Minga Digital is working to provide rural schools with access to modern computing facilities, thereby laying the groundwork for a future where quantum resources might also be accessible.

Further, enhancing educational opportunities stands as a crucial pillar in democratizing quantum technology. Various educational institutions are developing partnerships with technology companies and governmental bodies to create quantum literacy programs, designed to equip students across different demographics with the foundational knowledge to engage with quantum computing. For example, in South Africa, the National Institute for Theoretical and Computational Sciences (NITheCS) partners with universities and tech firms to integrate principles of quantum mechanics and computing into STEM curricula. By investing in education that prioritizes inclusivity, we form a bedrock upon which greater participation can be built.

Private enterprises also play a pivotal role. Companies like IBM and Google are making strides with initiatives like IBM's Qiskit, an open-source software development kit that allows individuals to program and experiment with quantum computers, regardless of their location. Moreover, competitions and hackathons organized by these tech giants are fostering environments where individuals from diverse backgrounds can collaborate, innovate, and contribute to the quantum landscape, further blurring the barriers traditionally drawn by socioeconomic status.

As we navigate these initiatives, practical examples surface, demonstrating how bridging the digital divide can manifest in meaningful change. Consider Nigeria's budding tech ecosystem, which has thrived due partly to partnerships with external organizations that focused on improving digital infrastructure and fostering local tech talent. By drawing resources towards quantum technologies, similar frameworks can pave the way for Africa's increased participation in global tech innovation, underscoring quantum computing's potential to transform economic prospects and foster international collaborations.

Thus, by critically examining the groundwork laid by current disparities, combined with specific strategies and initiatives aimed at bridging the gap, we paint a picture not merely of the obstacles to be overcome but of a futurescape rich with possibilities. Carrying forward these efforts, we prepare to explore how the collaborative nature and innovative spirit surrounding quantum computing promise to extend its reach toward a truly global audience. Transitioning into the next subchapter, we delve deeper into specific efforts that are turning this vision into reality, forging pathways toward a more inclusive quantum era.

Quantum Technology for All

As the burgeoning field of quantum computing moves closer to altering the landscape of technology as we know it, the priority of securing universal access becomes more pressing than ever. This subchapter delves into the concerted efforts being made across various sectors to democratize quantum technology. By fostering collaborative partnerships and innovation-driven initiatives, the aim is to render this revolutionary technology accessible to everyone, regardless of geography or socioeconomic status.

One of the fundamental pillars supporting the broad dissemination of quantum technology lies in comprehensive public and private collaborations. Governments around the globe recognize the transformative potential of quantum computing and are increasingly investing in strategic partnerships with educational institutions and private enterprises. For instance, the European Union's Quantum Flagship program, which spans over a decade with a billion-euro investment, aims to develop a competitive quantum industry, creating jobs and supporting key scientific advancements in the process. Such initiatives not only accelerate technical advancements but also decentralize resources and knowledge, enabling a more equitable technological future.

In the United States, the National Quantum Initiative Act serves as a pivotal mechanism to enhance quantum research and education. Launched with the purpose of bolstering national security and economic competitiveness, the act embodies a coordinated federal approach to accelerating quantum technology. Perhaps its most significant contribution is the encouragement of research hubs that integrate academic institutions and commercial entities. This hybrid approach mitigates the cost barriers associated with quantum computing by pooling expertise and resources for collective advancement.

A notable example of establishing access through partnerships can be seen in the collaboration between IBM and African universities. IBM has opened up its cutting-edge quantum computing platform to institutions across the continent, offering quantum courses and development programs. This initiative bridges the technological divide by providing students and researchers in Africa the tools they need to participate in quantum discovery, thus fostering an inclusive environment of global innovation.

Another innovative example is the Quantum Open Source Foundation, where developers and enthusiasts can contribute to a shared repository of quantum algorithms and software. The open-source model invites participation from anyone, anywhere, democratizing the development pipeline. This not only encourages widespread skill building but also capitalizes on the diverse problem-solving potential of global contributors.

To vividly illustrate the notion of "Quantum Technology for All," consider the case study of a rural high school in India that gained access to quantum resources through an outreach initiative by an international tech firm. Leveraging cloud-based quantum computing, students were able to run experiments that would traditionally be confined to well-funded labs. As a result, the students crafted a quantum machine learning model to optimize crop yields, showcasing the radical inclusivity and applicability of quantum technology in real-world scenarios.

Transitioning to the next subchapter, it becomes evident that widening access to quantum technologies undeniably raises important ethical questions. As we expand the reach of this advanced technology, it is critical to consider the moral quandaries that accompany its integration into various sectors. This will be explored in the following section dedicated to navigating the ethical landscape of the quantum realm.

Navigating Ethical Quandaries

As quantum computing weaves its threads into the fabric of modern life, it presents a unique spectrum of ethical challenges that demand careful navigation. Considered the powerhouse of computational potential, quantum technology has the ability to reshape industries and redefine societal norms. However, as with any formidable tool, its use poses critical ethical questions. How do we ensure that the immense power of quantum computing is wielded responsibly, safeguarding individual rights and societal welfare?

One of the most immediate ethical concerns is privacy. Quantum computing's unparalleled processing power threatens to render traditional encryption methods obsolete. If financial institutions, healthcare providers, or governmental bodies rush to adopt quantum technologies without proper safeguards, the result could be a catastrophic lapse in data security. Imagine a scenario where sensitive medical records, managed by quantum-enhanced systems, are vulnerable to quantum-powered breaches. Such a breach could lead to widespread misuse of personal data, putting millions at risk.

Another pressing issue is the impact on employment. Quantum technology, with its ability to solve complex problems at unheard-of speeds, is poised to revolutionize sectors such as pharmaceuticals, logistics, and artificial intelligence. However, it also foreshadows a substantial shift in the labor market. Jobs that depend on classical computing or traditional problem-solving may become obsolete, leading to widespread unemployment. Ethically, this compels us to strategize ways to retrain and upskill the workforce, ensuring that the human capital transitions smoothly into roles that harness the potential of quantum enhancements.

To navigate these ethical quandaries, we must adopt a structured framework for decision-making. One approach could involve adopting the principles of techno-ethics, which emphasize a balance between technological innovation and moral responsibility. Collaborative efforts among policymakers, technologists, and ethicists are pivotal in formulating guidelines that respect individual privacy, provide equitable opportunities in the job market, and promote fairness in technology distribution. For example, initiatives that involve regulatory bodies establishing quantum ethics committees could be instrumental. These committees would be tasked with continuously evaluating and updating ethical guidelines as the technology evolves, ensuring all stakeholders are aligned with the ethical norms.

A practical illustration of these concepts can be observed

in the European Union's approach to quantum ethics. The EU has been proactive in establishing research programs that explicitly address ethical considerations in quantum computing. By fostering an environment of open dialogue and cross-disciplinary collaboration, the EU aims to ensure that quantum advancements align with societal values. This has resulted in initiatives that prioritize equitable access to quantum resources, privacy preservation, and employment reskilling programs. Such examples underscore the importance of anticipatory governance —addressing ethical implications proactively rather than reactively.

As we continue to grapple with these ethical dilemmas, the focus remains on ensuring that quantum technology evolves in a manner that benefits humanity as a whole. This undertaking involves more than just understanding the technology itself; it demands a keen awareness of its ripple effects on society and a robust commitment to safeguarding ethical boundaries.

Ensuring Responsible Innovation

As quantum computing continues its rapid evolution, ensuring responsible innovation becomes not just an option but an imperative. Just as with other groundbreaking technologies, the promise of quantum computing is tempered by potential pitfalls that require careful management. To navigate this nascent landscape, we must draw on lessons learned from historical technological advancements, emphasizing the importance of ethical guidelines, regulatory frameworks, and collaborative efforts across disciplines.

At the forefront of responsible innovation is the establishment of clear regulatory frameworks. Analogous to the early days of the internet, where a lack of regulation led to growing pains, quantum computing must be steered by robust policies that anticipate ethical dilemmas and mitigate risks. For instance, quantum cryptography has the potential to revolutionize data security, but without proper guidelines, it could also facilitate unprecedented breaches of privacy. Agencies such as the National Institute of Standards and Technology (NIST) are already developing post-quantum cryptography standards, showcasing a proactive approach to defining secure paths forward.

The engagement of ethical guidelines cannot be understated. These guidelines serve as beacons, illuminating the ethical pathways navigated by researchers and developers in the quantum domain. Consider the dual-use nature of quantum technology, where innovations intended for beneficial uses could also be co-opted for harm. Here, the involvement of interdisciplinary ethics boards is crucial. By integrating perspectives from computer science, philosophy, and law, these boards can preemptively address ethical challenges, much like the ethical boards that govern biotechnological advancements.

Industry standards also play a pivotal role in ensuring that quantum technology evolves responsibly. Standards not only foster innovation by providing a level playing field but also promote safety by ensuring interoperability and compatibility across systems. The Quantum Industry Consortium, for example, has been instrumental in gathering stakeholders from various sectors to develop common standards, ensuring that advancements in quantum technology are aligned with societal needs and values.

One cannot overlook the importance of cross-disciplinary collaboration in this endeavor. The challenges and opportunities presented by quantum technologies are multidisciplinary, requiring input from various fields to create a balanced approach to innovation. Partnerships between academia, government, and industry ensure that diverse perspectives inform the responsible development of quantum technologies. This collaborative model is evidenced by initiatives like the European Quantum Flagship program, which unites academic researchers, policymakers, and industry leaders to drive quantum innovation with an eye towards societal benefits.

To ground these principles in practice, let us examine the framework applied in the European Union's General Data Protection Regulation (GDPR). Although it pertains primarily to digital data privacy, the GDPR represents a pioneering model of regulatory governance that balances innovation needs with societal protections. Its comprehensive approach to privacy and data management provides valuable insights into constructing frameworks for quantum technology—ensuring that while the technology advances, societal values such as privacy and security remain protected.

As we turn our focus to the broader societal implications of quantum computing in the following subchapter, consider the potential roles and responsibilities each stakeholder has in shaping this technology. Through responsible innovation, society stands on the brink of a technological transformation that respects both progress and preservation.

The Societal Impact of Quantum Technology

As we stand at the precipice of a quantum revolution, it is crucial to anticipate and understand the societal transformations that quantum computing will unleash across multiple arenas. This revolutionary technology holds the promise of addressing global challenges from climate modeling to complex data encryption, yet it also heralds new paradigms in economic frameworks, cultural dynamics, and social interactions. The societal impacts of quantum technology are multifaceted, presenting a complex tapestry of opportunities and responsibilities that must be navigated thoughtfully.

One of the most profound impacts of quantum computing is its potential to revolutionize industries through unprecedented levels of computational power. In fields such as pharmaceuticals, quantum computing has the capability to expedite drug discovery by enabling simulations of molecular interactions that are currently impossible to perform with classical computers. This transformation could lead to rapid advancements in medicine and healthcare, potentially making cures for diseases not only more accessible but also more customizable to individual genetic profiles. Such innovations, however, come with the challenge of ensuring equitable access to these medical breakthroughs globally, urging us to consider ethical frameworks that ensure inclusive benefits from these advancements.

In addition to scientific breakthroughs, quantum computing is poised to transform economic structures. As quantum technologies reshape industries, they will also redefine employment landscapes, requiring a workforce equipped with new skills in quantum theory, programming, and data analysis. This evolution calls for educational institutions and training programs to adapt rapidly, creating curricula that prepare future generations for participation in a quantum-enabled economy. Governments and businesses worldwide must collaborate to ensure that the benefits of quantum advancements do not concentrate in the hands of a few but rather diffuse equitably across all layers of society.

Culturally, the infusion of quantum technology into daily life promises to redefine our understanding of the universe and our place within it. The philosophical implications of quantum mechanics—challenges to classical notions of reality, causality, and linearity—are likely to resonate beyond the scientific community, influencing literature, art, and human self-conception. For example, quantum principles might inspire novel narratives in storytelling, offering new lenses through which to view the interconnectedness and complexity of human experiences. Such cultural shifts will necessitate a dialogue that acknowledges and navigates the diverse perspectives and implications of an increasingly quantum-aware society.

Socially, the deployment of quantum technology holds the potential to both enhance and disrupt human interactions. Quantum advancements could bring about unprecedented developments in secure communications, but they may also amplify existing privacy concerns. As quantum cryptography evolves, it prompts a reconsideration of privacy rights and data protection measures in a world where traditional encryption methods may no longer suffice. Stakeholders must work to balance the promise of enhanced security with the imperative of safeguarding individual freedoms, advocating for responsible digital citizenship and ethical data stewardship.

To illustrate these potential impacts, consider the case of the Australian government's collaborative initiative with academia and private enterprises, aimed at positioning Australia as a leader in quantum technology. By establishing the Sydney Quantum Academy, they provide scholars and industry professionals with resources and networks to advance quantum research and entrepreneurship. This program exemplifies how a strategic approach can enable an entire nation to harness the societal benefits of quantum technology, fostering economic growth, cultural enrichment, and social cohesion.

By nurturing a comprehensive dialogue among technology developers, policymakers, and citizens, we can better equip society to navigate the quantum era's challenges and opportunities. This collective effort encourages us to envision not only the technological transformations ahead but the societal enhancements quantum computing promises to deliver. As we transition toward the chapter's final analysis, these insights emphasize the integral role of strategic planning and ethical considerations in shaping a future where quantum innovations benefit all of humanity.

As we conclude on the theme of democratizing technology, it becomes clear that embracing the quantum revolution involves far more than advancing technical prowess—it represents a societal shift toward equitable innovation and ethical stewardship. Throughout this chapter, we have navigated the precarious balance between opportunity and challenge: the digital divide that threatens to exclude many, the initiatives aimed at nurturing inclusivity, and the ethical dilemmas that accompany technological advancement. These insights illuminate the profound responsibilities we bear as guardians of this nascent domain.

By examining current disparities and highlighting collaborative ventures, we've sketched a blueprint for a more inclusive future, where quantum technologies empower rather than alienate. Our discussions around ethical considerations reiterate the necessity for vigilant oversight and moral foresight, ensuring that quantum advancements align with societal values and needs. We've explored the contours of responsible innovation, anchored by historical precedents, which guide us toward robust policies and industry standards indispensable for sustainable progress.

Looking toward the horizon, the societal implications of quantum computing beckon us to envisage a redefined world—one where technology serves to elevate human potential and deepen social equity. As we prepare to advance into the next chapter, let us carry forward the imperative to harness quantum technology responsibly, with an unwavering commitment to ethical integrity and universal benefit.

In the following chapters, we will delve deeper into how

these technological and ethical foundations can catalyze transformative impacts across diverse sectors, from healthcare to communication, offering a glimpse into the tangible realities of tomorrow. Let this exploration inspire you to ponder how these innovations might intersect with your personal and professional landscapes, fueling your role in this extraordinary frontier of possibility.

CHAPTER 8: BUILDING A QUANTUM WORKFORCE

In the liminal space between the theoretical musings of quantum mechanics and the tangible realities of modern technology lies a frontier teeming with potential—quantum computing. As industries worldwide pivot to embrace the unprecedented capabilities of this paradigm-shifting technology, the cultivation of a specialized workforce has emerged as both a challenge and an opportunity. The eighth chapter of our exploration into this new technological era, "Building a Quantum Workforce," seeks to unravel the intricate tapestry of demand and education, collaboration and innovation, that will define the quantum era.

To understand the impetus behind this workforce revolution, we first delve into the rising demand for quantum expertise. As quantum breakthroughs continue to break traditional limits of computation and problem-solving, myriad industries—ranging from cryptography to healthcare—are on the hunt for individuals who can translate abstract quantum theories into actionable solutions. It is a quest for the rare polymath who can straddle the divide between scientific inquiry and industrial application, a theme explored thoroughly in our opening subchapter.

Seeding a new generation of quantum-savvy professionals begins with transforming education systems. Universities and research institutions worldwide are architecting sophisticated programs to equip future trailblazers with the requisite knowledge and skills. As we embark into our second subchapter, we will navigate through these dynamic educational frameworks, where the old silos of disciplines are being dismantled in favor of interdisciplinary curriculums that merge physics, computer science, and engineering. Here, the burgeoning role of online platforms as democratizers of this specialized knowledge, opening doors to diverse and often underrepresented groups, will also be in focus.

The synergy between academia and industry forms the lifeblood of technological advancement. In our third subchapter, we will spotlight the symbiotic partnerships that have sprouted, fostering environments ripe for collaboration and exploration. These alliances not only drive the research frontier forward but also imbue students with practical experience, needed to navigate the nuances of real-world quantum applications.

The prospects awaiting qualified individuals in the quantum realm are both fascinating and multifaceted. Our fourth subchapter will guide you through the myriad career pathways available, from research scientists to systems engineers. We will illuminate these paths with case studies of professionals who have successfully carved niches in the quantum sector, while providing aspiring talents with valuable insights and inspiration to chart their own journeys.

Finally, as we look towards the horizon, the closing subchapter will address the necessity of perpetual learning and adaptability to remain at the forefront of quantum innovation. Preparing for a quantum future involves not only the honing of technical skills but also the development of an ethical framework that ensures quantum's benefits are widely shared. This exploration sets the stage for further discussions on the evolving roles and responsibilities of the quantum workforce in shaping society.

With these threads interwoven, "Building a Quantum Workforce" beckons you to ponder the profound challenges and opportunities that lie ahead. It invites you to journey deeper into a world where the impossible begins to crack under the pressure of human ingenuity and collective action—where you too might play a part in shaping a quantum future.

The Demand for Quantum Expertise

In an era where technology evolves at breakneck speed, the ascent of quantum computing stands as a lodestar for the future, promising to redefine industries and economies globally. The genesis of this transformative wave lies in the burgeoning demand for quantum expertise—a challenge that rings like a clarion call across the diverse landscapes of technology, finance, healthcare, and beyond. As breakthroughs in quantum technology snowball, the quest for adept professionals who can metamorphose theoretical constructs into applicable solutions has never been more pressing.

Quantum computing, with its roots steeped in the enigmatic realms of quantum mechanics, offers unprecedented computational power capable of solving complex problems that remain intractable for classical computers. This potential is not lost on industry giants. In fields as diverse as cryptography, material science, and drug discovery, the need for quantum expertise is swiftly expanding. Companies such as IBM, Google, and Microsoft are racing to develop practical quantum solutions, illuminating the urgent need for skilled practitioners who can navigate this intricate terrain.

Consider the financial sector—a domain where milliseconds can dictate fortune or failure. Quantum computing promises to revolutionize this industry by performing risk analyses, complex optimizations, and digital encryption at speeds inconceivable to classical systems. The recruitment frenzy for quantum-ready talent is already palpable in this space, as financial institutions seek out those capable of pioneering quantum-driven trading algorithms.

Simultaneously, the healthcare industry vies for quantum prowess to decode the complexities of biological systems. Quantum computing holds the keys to revolutionizing drug discovery by simulating molecular interactions at an unprecedented scale and specificity. As laboratories and pharmaceutical companies converge on this frontier, the demand for quantum-savvy scientists and engineers continues to escalate.

Moreover, addressing climate change through advanced technologies has become a global imperative. Quantum computing's ability to optimize logistical systems or model atmospheric changes paves the way for environmental and energy sectors to leverage its potential, thus requiring professionals adept at translating quantum simulations into actionable strategies.

As we observe these seismic shifts, it is crucial to understand the current and projected workforce needs that underpin this quantum revolution. A recent report from the consulting firm McKinsey highlights a looming skills gap, forecasting that the demand for quantum experts will triple in the next decade. These insights challenge educational institutions and corporations alike to align their training and hiring strategies with this anticipated surge.

A salient example of industry-wide adaptation is the emergence of quantum incubator programs within tech companies like Rigetti Computing in California. By fostering environments where industry veterans mentor emerging talent, Rigetti ensures that theoretical brilliance is paired with industry acumen, thus nurturing a new breed of quantum professionals.

As we transition to the next subchapter, the focus will shift to the educational pathways being forged to satiate this demand for quantum expertise. These pathways are designed to cultivate the skills necessary for thriving in an era defined by quantum possibilities. Our journey continues as we delve into the ways institutions worldwide are sculpting curricula that interlace scientific rigor with innovative technology—a harmonization imperative for tomorrow's leaders in the quantum cosmos.

Educational Pathways to Quantum Proficiency

As the relentless wave of quantum advancements reshapes industries, the academic world is rapidly evolving to meet the burgeoning demand for quantum expertise. While traditional fields of study laid essential groundwork, a new era of interdisciplinary education promises to forge the workforce capable of navigating this quantum-driven landscape. Bridging the sciences with technology, universities and research institutions worldwide are pioneering educational pathways that promise to equip learners with the requisite quantum acumen.

At the forefront of this evolution, several leading academic institutions are developing robust programs that transcend traditional pedagogical models. These curricula ingeniously integrate physics, computer science, and engineering, recognizing that a holistic understanding is crucial when dealing with the multidimensional aspects of quantum computing. An exemplar of such integration is the University of Waterloo's Institute for Quantum Computing in Canada, which melds theoretical research with practical application across physics and computer science domains. Similarly, MIT's Center for Quantum Engineering pursues interdisciplinary approaches, enabling students to engage with quantum mechanics and computational techniques harmoniously.

Beyond institutional walls, online education platforms stand as formidable gateways to democratizing access to quantum knowledge. By offering courses developed in partnership with leading quantum experts, platforms like Coursera and edX dismantle geographical barriers, allowing diverse populations to immerse themselves in quantum studies. These platforms enable aspiring quantum professionals from around the globe, regardless of their financial or location constraints, to develop skills in quantum algorithms, quantum circuits, and quantum information theory, often at their own pace.

In parallel, research initiatives are catalyzed by collaborative networks that draw on global ingenuity and perspectives. Programs like the Quantum Information and Computation Initiative at the University of Tokyo and the Quantum Flagship initiative in the European Union illustrate a cross-continental commitment to shared learning and advancement in quantum sciences. These collaborations not only empower students with a robust academic footing but also expose them to international perspectives that enhance the richness of their educational experience.

To illustrate the practical application of these educational pathways, consider the journey of Susan Li, a physics undergraduate fascinated by quantum potentials. Inspired by a seminar from the National University of Singapore's Centre for Quantum Technologies, Susan proactively enrolled in an online quantum computing series. Successfully completing these courses allowed her to partake in a research internship at a leading tech firm specializing in quantum software. Susan's journey exemplifies how combining institutional learning with online resources can propel students into the heart of quantum research and innovation, turning educational pursuits into tangible career opportunities.

In training the pioneers of tomorrow, educational frameworks tailored to quantum computing are creating a magnetic pole for talent worldwide. Yet, as we delve further into the intricacies of building a quantum workforce, it becomes evident that these educational advancements must be complemented by strategic partnerships, the topic of our next subchapter, which examines the symbiotic relationships between academia and industry driving the quantum revolution forward.

Partnerships Between Industry and Academia

As we delve into the collaborative landscape of quantum computing, one cannot overlook the symbiotic relationship blossoming between industry and academic institutions. These partnerships are not merely joint ventures but rather pioneering alliances driving the forefront of quantum technology innovation. By integrating academic rigor with industry pragmatism, such collaborations create a fertile ground for groundbreaking research and skill development that benefits both realms.

At the core of these partnerships is a shared vision of fostering innovation. For example, the IBM Quantum Network illustrates how corporate and academic entities can unite to accelerate advancements in quantum research. This network connects over 170 organizations across multiple sectors, including academic institutions like Stanford University and MIT. By providing access to IBM's quantum computers, the initiative enables academic researchers to run experiments on real quantum devices, thereby transcending the limitations of theoretical simulations.

Furthermore, these alliances are instrumental in generating significant advancements in quantum algorithms and applications. The collaboration between Microsoft and the University of Sydney exemplifies this dynamic. They have jointly developed quantum software tools designed to optimize quantum computations, laying the groundwork for practical applications from cryptography to complex logistical models. This type of cooperative effort not only pushes the boundaries of what is achievable with quantum computing but also equips students with firsthand experience using cutting-edge technologies.

One of the most salient aspects of these partnerships is their role in cultivating an employable workforce. By allowing students to directly interface with industry leaders, educational institutions create opportunities that transcend the traditional classroom experience. Students benefit from internships and collaborative research projects, which provide invaluable practical insights and industry connections. Google's Qubit Initiative with the University of California, Berkeley, is a prime example, where students work alongside Google engineers, gaining exposure to real-world quantum challenges and learning how to apply their academic knowledge to solve pressing industry problems.

For instance, consider the case of Dr. Elena Lopez, who began her journey as a physics student at UC Berkeley. Through a collaborative internship with Google, she was able to work on optimizing error correction algorithms for quantum computers. This hands-on experience not only enriched her understanding but also led to her permanent role as a quantum engineer at Google, where she continues to contribute to developing scalable quantum solutions. Dr. Lopez's journey underscores the tangible impact that academic-industry partnerships can have on career trajectories within the quantum field.

As we transition to exploring career pathways in the quantum realm, it becomes evident that such collaborative ecosystems play a crucial role in shaping the professional landscape. The exposure and experience gained through these partnerships empower aspiring professionals to venture confidently into the dynamic world of quantum computing. This groundwork sets aspiring minds on a path to explore various roles within the field, from research and development to software engineering and beyond.

Career Pathways in the
Quantum Realm

The quantum landscape is a burgeoning frontier, ripe with diverse career opportunities for those equipped with the right expertise. As quantum computing ventures from the theoretical into the practical, an array of roles is becoming available, bridging the gap between nascent technology and transformative application.

At the core of the quantum workforce are research scientists, the pioneers pushing the boundaries of what's possible. These individuals delve deep into the intricacies of quantum mechanics, seeking new algorithms and materials that can exploit quantum phenomena. One illustrative example is the work being done at Google AI Quantum, where researchers are developing quantum algorithms for near-term quantum computers, aiming to solve problems that were previously thought intractable.

Beyond research, algorithm developers are also in high demand. These professionals translate quantum principles into executable programs that harness the unique capabilities of quantum processors. Consider IBM, which has assembled a team of talented developers working on Qiskit, an open-source software development kit that simplifies quantum computing programming. This initiative not only advances IBM's quantum offerings but also nurtures a community of developers who contribute to the ecosystem's growth.

Systems engineers play a critical role in the practical deployment of quantum systems. They are responsible for designing and maintaining the complex infrastructure required to support quantum operations. Rigetti Computing serves as a prime example, employing systems engineers who ensure seamless operation by overseeing components from refrigeration units to error-correcting codes.

Quantum software specialists, while newer on the scene, represent an essential facet of the workforce. These professionals adapt existing software paradigms to the quantum context, designing tools that facilitate ease of use and integration. Xanadu, a leader in photonics-based quantum technologies, employs software specialists to develop applications leveraging their Xanadu Cloud platform, offering clients user-friendly quantum solutions.

Highlighting the diverse skill sets beneficial in the quantum industry, let us profile Maria Gonzales, a physicist turned quantum consultant. Maria began her career in academia, earning a doctorate in quantum physics before transitioning to a role at a leading technology consultancy. She leverages her foundational knowledge in quantum mechanics to advise Fortune 500 companies on integrating quantum strategies, underscoring the importance of interdisciplinary applications in her work.

Furthermore, as the quantum field is still forming, entrepreneurial opportunities abound. Startups focused on niche applications, such as quantum cryptography or quantum error correction, invite professionals to bring innovation to the marketplace, cultivating an environment where new ideas can flourish.

Each of these roles exemplifies the potential for impactful careers within the quantum realm, highlighting the importance of a varied skill set—from deep scientific understanding to hands-on engineering and creative problem-solving. The rapidly advancing technologies offer opportunities for continual growth, attracting those with the agility to adapt and thrive.

As professionals and aspiring experts navigate these pathways, real-world experiences, such as internships and collaborative projects, will form crucial stepping stones. One prominent initiative is the Microsoft Quantum Network, which connects industry and academia, allowing students to gain practical exposure under the mentorship of leading quantum scientists. These collaborations provide not only skill development but also networking opportunities that can yield long-term career benefits.

With this understanding of the versatile career paths available, as well as the practical steps to pursue them, the next logical focus centers on preparing for a future deeply interwoven with quantum advancements. Ensuring readiness for this future involves not only fostering technical skills but also adopting a mindset oriented towards continuous learning and adaptation. Let's turn our attention to envisioning the strategies necessary to thrive in the quantum-driven world of tomorrow.

Preparing for a Quantum Future

Gazing into the future of a quantum-driven world necessitates a careful examination of not just the technologies that will shape tomorrow, but also the people who will drive these innovations forward. As quantum computing begins to permeate various aspects of society, there is a compelling need for a workforce that is not only skilled in the technical nuances of quantum systems but also adaptable, ethically conscious, and committed to lifelong learning.

The Imperative of Continuous Learning

In the rapidly evolving landscape of quantum technology, the only constant is change. Consequently, continuous learning becomes an indispensable strategy for staying relevant in this dynamic field. Professionals and aspiring students alike must embrace the idea that education does not conclude with formal schooling but is an ongoing process that extends throughout one's career. Industry-related workshops, online courses, and technical forums offer platforms for knowledge enhancement and skill development, ensuring that individuals remain at the cutting edge of technological advancements.

Consider the case of Dr. Emily Chang, a research scientist whose journey illustrates the power of adaptability and learning. After completing her doctorate in quantum mechanics, Dr. Chang faced a market where the applications of her research were just beginning to emerge. Rather than wait for opportunities, she proactively enhanced her understanding of computer science and machine learning through online courses. Her commitment to learning allowed her to transition into the field of quantum algorithms, eventually leading to her current role at a leading quantum computing firm where she collaborates on groundbreaking research. Dr. Chang's story exemplifies how staying curious and continually expanding one's skill set can open doors to unexpected opportunities in the quantum realm.

Ethical Considerations in Workforce Development

As the quantum workforce grows, there arises a necessity to instill a strong ethical grounding in its practitioners. Quantum technologies hold the promise of solving complex problems but also present challenges related to privacy, security, and equitable access. Educators and industry leaders must therefore integrate ethical considerations into scientific and technical training programs to prepare professionals who are not only capable but conscientious.

Institutions are beginning to address this by incorporating ethics courses into their curricula for quantum studies. These classes explore scenarios where ethical dilemmas may surface in quantum applications, prompting students to think critically about the societal implications of their work. For instance, discussions around the potential misuse of quantum cryptography in government surveillance serve as a springboard for understanding the importance of ethical decision-making.

Realizing the Societal Promise of Quantum Advancements

Building a quantum-savvy workforce is not solely about meeting industry needs; it also involves ensuring that the transformative benefits of quantum technology are widespread. To that end, efforts must be made to democratize access to education and resources, particularly in underserved communities. Initiatives such as scholarships for women and minorities in STEM fields, alongside community outreach programs, can foster a diverse array of perspectives within the quantum domain.

A practical example is the Quantum Leap Community Project, a non-profit organization that partners with tech companies to provide free educational workshops on quantum computing to high schools in underrepresented areas. By engaging young minds early and inclusively, the project aims to spark interest in quantum sciences and cultivate a future talent pool capable of exploring and expanding the potential of quantum technologies.

Preparing for a quantum future involves a synergistic approach that combines lifelong learning, ethical mindfulness, and inclusivity. By equipping the workforce with these tools, we can navigate the challenges and harness the opportunities of a quantum-powered tomorrow. As we transition to the chapter's conclusion, we will explore how these strategies collectively fortify the foundation for sustained growth and innovation in the quantum era.

As we conclude this enlightening journey through Chapter 8, "Building a Quantum Workforce," we find ourselves standing at the threshold of an exciting era replete with opportunity and promise. The burgeoning demand for quantum expertise is reshaping the employment landscape, creating a fertile ground for those ready to harness its disruptive potential. We've explored how educational institutions are rising to the challenge, crafting innovative pathways to prepare a new generation of quantum-savvy professionals who will be instrumental in bridging theory with practice.

Our investigation into partnerships between academia and industry has illuminated how crucial these alliances are in fostering environments rich with innovation and practical experience. Such collaborations are not only advancing quantum research and development but are also providing students with the early exposure necessary to excel in this dynamic field.

Career pathways we've examined reveal a vast array of roles, each requiring a blend of unique skill sets. The stories of individuals successfully navigating these careers underscore the necessity of adaptability and continuous learning—skills that will be essential in surfing the quantum wave.

Finally, as we look forward to a quantum future, it becomes clear that building a workforce ready for such transformative change involves a thoughtful balance between technological prowess and ethical mindfulness. To ensure equity and preparedness, we must embrace these changes with a strategic mind and an open heart.

As the book unfolds further, we will delve deeper into the revolutionary impacts quantum computing promises to unleash across diverse sectors. Prepare to explore the societal shifts and philosophical questions emanating from this technological frontier. As you step into the next chapter, let the foundations laid here inspire you to not only envision but actively participate in shaping a future that is on the brink of redefinition.

CHAPTER 9: CURRENT CHALLENGES AND MISCONCEPTIONS

As we venture deeper into the realm of quantum computing, it is essential to confront the current challenges that persistently shape its journey and how they affect our understanding and expectations. Chapter 9 opens a window onto a landscape riddled with intricate hurdles and widespread misconceptions, offering readers a profound insight into the reality underpinning this revolutionary technology.

In the world of quantum computing, the path to progress is seldom a straight line. The very technologies poised to redefine the future face an array of formidable technical challenges. In the first subchapter, "Navigating the Technical Hurdles," we delve into the heart of these complexities. From the relentless battle with high error rates in quantum operations to the critical necessity of maintaining quantum coherence, and the daunting task of scaling quantum systems, each obstacle presents not just a challenge, but an opportunity for innovation. By untangling these technical knots, the stage is set for a deeper understanding of why certain quantum solutions remain in the theoretical pipeline and what inventive methods are being crafted to transcend these barriers.

Moving beyond the tangible realm, "Theoretical Conundrums and their Impacts" takes us into the abstract yet crucial domain of theory. Here, we explore the unsolved puzzles that quantum computing presents to the scientific community. From the quest to optimize quantum algorithms to the intricate dance of harmonizing quantum mechanics with other scientific tenets, these theoretical challenges are not mere academic exercises. They are the keys to unlocking quantum computing's full potential, influencing practical applications and steering the direction of future research. The dialogue between theory and practice emerges as a driving force in this unfolding narrative.

Yet, amid these genuine challenges, misconceptions abound. In "Misconceptions about Quantum Capabilities," we confront the myths that pervade popular discourse. Quantum computing is shrouded in a mystique that sometimes leads to extravagant expectations—from the premature proclamation of quantum supremacy to the reckless assumption that classical computers will instantaneously become relics of the past. By dissecting these fallacies, we ground ourselves in a realistic appraisal of current capabilities and identify what lies feasible on the horizon.

This chapter also examines "Bridging Public Perception and Scientific Reality," highlighting the significant gap between what is often portrayed in the media and the scientific truth. Here, we delve into the responsibility shared by scientists, technologists, and communicators to ensure that public curiosity is met with accurate information rather than driven by hype. Richard Drayton, with his commitment to illuminating the nuances of quantum technology, seeks to foster a well-informed public, capable of engaging with these concepts intelligently.

Finally, "Preparing for the Inevitable Challenges Ahead" brings us to the strategic foresight necessary for navigating the turbulent waters of technological evolution. It calls for interdisciplinary collaboration, investment in research, and the adaptation of educational models to prepare for a quantum future. While acknowledging the inherent challenges of technological revolutions, it celebrates their role as catalysts for growth, setting the stage for the visionary propositions that await in the subsequent narrative.

As we journey through Chapter 9, we invite you to explore these challenges and misconceptions, equipping yourself with the knowledge to not only understand quantum computing's present landscape but also navigate its promising yet demanding future.

Navigating the Technical Hurdles

In the rapidly evolving domain of quantum computing, technical challenges form a formidable barrier to the realization of its full potential. As we journey through these hurdles, it becomes evident that the path to quantum supremacy is not only a test of human ingenuity but also a testament to our unwavering pursuit of knowledge. Each obstacle provides an opportunity for innovative approaches that could unlock unprecedented computational capabilities.

One of the primary challenges is the persistent issue of error rates in quantum operations. In classical computing, a binary system offers a level of stability that results in remarkably low error rates. However, quantum bits, or qubits, exist in a state of superposition, where they can represent both 0 and 1 simultaneously. This delicate state renders them susceptible to interference from external forces, leading to high error rates. Imagine a classical marathon where each runner battles only external weather conditions, whereas quantum researchers contend with ever-changing, unpredictable forces affecting each step they take. This raises a critical question: how do we ensure error correction in such a dynamically unstable environment?

Several innovative strategies are emerging to address these error rates. Error-correcting codes are in development, utilizing additional qubits to detect and rectify errors without disturbing the computation's integrity. Although promising, these solutions require substantial computational resources, which simultaneously highlights a second challenge facing the field: scalability. Quantum systems need to transition from handling tens of qubits to managing thousands, without a proportional increase in errors. For instance, Google's Sycamore processor, which momentarily achieved quantum supremacy, demonstrated how achieving scalable quantum advantage requires significant advancement in both hardware and algorithmic design.

Maintaining quantum coherence is another significant hurdle. Coherence is essential for the effective execution of quantum algorithms; it is the measure of a qubit maintaining its quantum state over time. Loss of coherence, akin to a performer losing balance on a tightrope, can lead to the collapse of superpositions, rendering quantum processes unreliable. To address this, researchers are exploring advanced materials and environments, such as cryogenic systems, that can sustain coherence for longer periods. Strategies like creating sheltered, vibration-resistant environments contribute to minimizing decoherence.

Understanding the technical barriers in quantum computing also invites us to consider real-world applications where overcoming these challenges could revolutionize industries. Take, for example, pharmaceuticals. The development of new drugs involves calculating molecular interactions with extreme precision. Classical computers find such tasks daunting due to the sheer number of variables involved. Quantum computers, by solving complex equations almost instantaneously, hold the potential to accelerate drug discovery processes exponentially. Policymakers, researchers, and businesses alike could witness faster, more efficient pathways to tackling diseases, saving lives and resources.

To illustrate these concepts in practice, we can look at the partnership between IBM and Daimler for advancing electric vehicle batteries. The collaboration leverages quantum computers to model and simulate the chemical processes in lithium-sulfur cells, a potential alternative to the conventional lithium-ion batteries. Through intricate simulation capabilities, quantum computers can explore new material combinations more efficiently than classical computers, potentially leading to batteries that offer higher capacity and longer life at reduced costs.

As we move forward, understanding and mitigating these technical challenges not only propels quantum technology itself but influences broader technological and industrial landscapes. The journey through these obstacles lays the groundwork for engaging with the subsequent theoretical conundrums, leading to a deeper comprehension of quantum computing's intricate and fascinating universe.

Theoretical Conundrums and Their Impacts

As we transition from the raw technicalities of quantum systems, our lens shifts to the ethereal abstractions—the theoretical conundrums that continue to perplex some of the finest minds in quantum computing. While quantum computers tantalize us with their promise, they also unravel into a labyrinth of theoretical challenges that must be met before they can reach their full potential. Understanding these challenges provides us with the context to appreciate the intricate dance between theory and application, a fundamental aspect for anyone who wishes to tread this frontier.

At the core of these theoretical puzzles is the optimization of quantum algorithms. In classical computing, we take for granted algorithms that drive everything from artificial intelligence to e-commerce. In the quantum realm, however, crafting algorithms that harness the bizarre properties of superposition and entanglement remains a relentless pursuit. Consider Shor's algorithm, which promises exponential speed-up in factorizing large numbers, a key operation in cryptography. While its theoretical efficiency is well-documented, real-world deployment is hampered by the noise and decoherence present in contemporary quantum computers. Therefore, researchers must incessantly refine and invent new algorithms that are robust against such imperfections, which demands a deep, theoretical understanding of both quantum mechanics and computational theory.

Another towering challenge is the reconciliation of quantum mechanics with other domains of theoretical physics, especially when considering the integration with classical computational frameworks. This challenge is emblematic of the broader quest to unify physics, as traditional models often fall short of describing phenomena when quantum effects are predominant. For instance, finding common ground between quantum computing principles and classical thermodynamics is essential for developing error-correction methods that are efficient and scalable.

The implications of these theoretical challenges reverberate through the practical applications of quantum computing. Industries investing in quantum technology face a complex terrain, where algorithmic breakthroughs are a prerequisite for realizing industry-specific applications. Take, for example, the pharmaceutical industry's interest in quantum simulations for drug discovery. While theoretically feasible, current algorithms must evolve to optimize simulations in a quantum environment before they can revolutionize molecular modeling and dramatically reduce drug development timelines.

Furthermore, these theoretical endeavors guide the future path of quantum research. They direct investments and policy-making in technological development and influence educational strategies meant to produce the next generation of quantum scientists. Theoretical advancements fundamentally shape how quantum technologies are perceived, developed, and eventually integrated into societal frameworks.

To illustrate the critical role of theoretical innovations in advancing quantum computing, let's examine a practical development: the Quantum Approximate Optimization Algorithm (QAOA). This algorithm exemplifies how theoretical insights directly impact applied scenarios. QAOA is designed to tackle optimization problems across logistics, finance, and other sectors. Although still in a nascent stage, it is actively being tested on existing quantum devices, showcasing how theoretical advances in algorithm development are paving the way for practical, real-world solutions.

Such examples underscore the necessity of continued theoretical exploration, linking directly to the practical considerations surrounding quantum technologies. As we further investigate the landscape of quantum computing, understanding theory's role becomes instrumental in overcoming misconceptions and clarifying public expectations—a discussion we will now explore in the subsequent subchapter.

Misconceptions about Quantum Capabilities

In the burgeoning field of quantum computing, where every advancement seems to herald a dawn of new possibilities, clear understanding often falls victim to enthralling but exaggerated narratives. As quantum computing continues to capture the public imagination, it is increasingly important to parse reality from conjecture, especially in a landscape where predictions are abundant, and definitive timelines are few and far between.

One prevalent misconception revolves around the much-discussed milestone of quantum supremacy. This term, popularized by a 2019 announcement from Google claiming they had achieved it, suggests that quantum computers can now perform tasks impossible for classical supercomputers. However, the specific task Google tackled was delicately chosen and not practically applicable beyond proving a conceptual point. The confusion arises when media touts quantum supremacy as a harbinger of a revolution replacing classical computing entirely. In practice, quantum supremacy represents a carefully crafted test rather than a practical milestone.

Furthermore, while the remarkable speedups promised by quantum algorithms, such as Shor's algorithm for factoring, indicate potential leaps in processing specific computational problems, it is incorrect to infer they will render classical computers obsolete. Many tasks, particularly those requiring precise numerical calculations, remain outside the suitable domain for quantum computers, where error-correction remains a profound challenge.

To help elucidate these concepts, consider the world of quantum cryptography and its application to secure communications. While it promises theoretically unbreakable encryption, current implementations are limited to relatively short transmission distances and expensive infrastructure investments, illustrating a chasm between theoretical potential and practical utility.

Real-world scenarios often shine a light on these descriptors. Take, for example, the pharmaceutical industry, a field frequently cited as a beneficiary of quantum technology. The promise is that quantum computers could model complex molecules, speeding up drug discovery and revolutionizing treatment options. However, at present, quantum simulations remain under development, largely due to a lack of qubits—the fundamental units of quantum information—capable of maintaining stability to perform their tasks reliably over necessary timescales.

Similarly, financial modeling is another domain that, on paper, stands to gain from quantum advancements. Quantum algorithms could, in theory, evaluate risk profiles or optimize large investment portfolios more efficiently than classical algorithms. Yet, the current status quo shows investment banks carefully evaluating the integration of quantum software into existing systems, mindful that while potentials are exciting, real-world deployments are not imminent.

These scenarios offer a grounded perspective: the ongoing necessity is not just inventing new capabilities but refining our understanding and managing expectations about what quantum computing can truly achieve today. Forging such clarity is crucial as the field progresses, aligning future investments with realistic timelines and ensuring that the quantum leap builds on a foundation of informed enthusiasm rather than hype-driven misconception.

The discussions surrounding the misconceptions of quantum computing capabilities contribute to a broader dialogue involving both scientists and the public. It sets the stage for our next exploration—bridging the gap between public perception and scientific reality of quantum computing. Here, we delve into how accurate communication can educate and empower an inquisitive public, transforming how new technologies are perceived, adopted, and utilized.

Bridging Public Perception and Scientific Reality

In the swiftly evolving domain of quantum computing, where speculation often outpaces reality, navigating the crisscross of public perception and scientific reality becomes an essential endeavor. The allure of quantum computing has captured the imagination of many, yet the journey from scientific breakthrough to practical application is intricate and requires careful articulation to align public expectations with scientific progress.

The media, with its sensational storytelling and compelling

headlines, plays an undeniable role in shaping the public's understanding. Often caught in the enthusiastic current of declaring the dawn of new technological eras, media representations can inadvertently embellish the capabilities of this nascent technology. It is not uncommon to encounter claims that suggest quantum computers will soon revolutionize every facet of life, from medicine to finance, at the mere flip of a switch. While optimistic visions serve to ignite public interest and investment, they can also foster misconceptions that challenge scientific integrity and lead to unrealistic expectations.

The responsibility of bridging this gap falls on the shoulders of scientists, technologists, and communicators who are well-versed in walking the tightrope between accessibility and accuracy. Authors like myself, Richard Drayton, hold the duty of translating complex scientific concepts into narratives that resonate with the general public without sacrificing truth for simplicity. It is imperative that we employ our storytelling skills not just to captivate, but to educate.

Creating a dialogue that addresses this disconnect begins with framing a realistic portrayal of where quantum computing stands today and where it is headed. When media headlines declare "Quantum Supremacy Achieved," it is our charge to explain the nuanced milestones such as Google's 2019 announcement, which, while historic, represents a narrow demonstration of superiority in a specific, highly controlled context rather than a sweeping conquest over classical computers.

To illustrate the importance of accurate communication, consider the case study of RSA encryption, a cryptographic protocol widely deemed unbreakable by classical computers within a reasonable time frame. Public fear escalated upon hearing quantum computers might easily break such codes, yet a practical quantum computer capable of this feat is still years, if not decades, away. By explaining the current technical limitations, like maintaining coherence in enough qubits to execute such tasks, we temper fear with fact and lay a groundwork for informed discourse.

Further, it is crucial to foster an environment where scientists and communicators collaboratively spearhead initiatives that inform and inspire without distortion. This means engaging with educational systems early, integrating quantum literacy into curricula to shift from a reactive to a proactive stance in science education. Public engagement events, accessible yet authoritative publications, and interdisciplinary workshops are all vital tools in recalibrating the public's expectations and informing them of the incremental, yet momentous progress being made.

In conclusion, the key lies in maintaining a balance between visionary possibilities and the sober rewrites of scientific reality. This ensures that enthusiasm for quantum computing remains grounded in facts and thereby sustains the momentum of research and development. As we move forward, the next subchapter will look at preparing for the inevitable challenges that lie ahead, exploring how proactive strategies can further enhance our understanding and application of quantum technology in the real world.

Preparing for the Inevitable Challenges Ahead

As we stand on the precipice of a quantum revolution, preparing for the inevitable challenges this next phase presents is not just a necessity, but an opportunity to harness the transformative power of quantum computing. This subchapter delves into the strategic frameworks and innovative mindsets required to address these challenges effectively.

Interdisciplinary collaboration emerges as a cornerstone in navigating the complexities of quantum computing. This field is intrinsically woven through the threads of physics, computer science, mathematics, engineering, and beyond. As quantum systems grow more sophisticated, the demand for collaborative efforts across these diverse domains intensifies. Companies like Google and IBM have already set a precedent by assembling cross-functional teams that include physicists, computer scientists, and engineers working in concert to push the boundaries of what is technologically feasible.

Continuous investment in research and development also stands as a pivotal strategy. For instance, national governments and private enterprises are increasingly channeling substantial resources into quantum research initiatives, recognizing the potential competitive edge quantum technology offers. These investments are essential not just for advancing hardware capabilities but also for exploring new algorithms that can unlock unprecedented efficiencies in data processing and problem-solving.

Moreover, there is an urgent need to adapt educational frameworks to cultivate a workforce equipped for quantum innovation. Universities and educational institutions are beginning to embed quantum computing into their curricula, often offering specialized degrees and training programs. The University of California, Berkeley, for example, has initiated courses that introduce students to both the theoretical underpinnings and practical applications of quantum technology, preparing a new generation of thinkers to tackle future challenges head-on.

Innovation thrives where challenges exist. The technological hurdles faced by quantum computing today serve as a catalyst for groundbreaking breakthroughs tomorrow. By encouraging an environment where experimentation and discovery are celebrated, institutions not only solve existing problems but also pave the way for unforeseen advancements. This approach was vividly demonstrated by the development of quantum error-correcting codes which, despite seeming infeasible at their inception, have become central to the pursuit of stable and functional quantum systems.

To illustrate the practical application of these strategies, consider the collaboration between pharmaceutical companies and quantum computing firms. These partnerships aim to revolutionize drug discovery by utilizing quantum algorithms to simulate molecular interactions at an unprecedented scale. Such collaborations epitomize how interdisciplinary teamwork and strategic investment can yield tangible outcomes, propelling industries into new realms of possibility.

This evolving landscape of quantum computing challenges us to engage not only our technical expertise but our imaginative capacities. By preparing thoughtfully and collaboratively, we are poised to steer this transformative technology toward a future where innovation is boundless and the realms of the possible are continually redefined. The chapter's final conclusions will extend these insights, considering the broader implications for society and the potential pathways that lie ahead.

As we conclude Chapter 9, "Current Challenges and Misconceptions," we stand at a pivotal moment in the journey of understanding quantum computing. We've traversed the complex landscape of technical hurdles, confronting error rates, coherence challenges, and the scalability issues that persist in our quest to harness quantum potential. Our exploration then transitioned to the theoretical realm, where the need to optimize quantum algorithms and connect with broader physical theories remains a formidable yet exciting challenge.

We clarified the capabilities of quantum computers, cutting through media exaggerations to depict an accurate view of their current and future roles. Recognizing the gap between public perception and scientific reality, we emphasized the vital responsibility shared by scientists and communicators to empower an informed audience, prepared to engage with new technologies thoughtfully.

Finally, we prepared for the inevitable challenges that lie ahead by highlighting the necessity of interdisciplinary cooperation, continued investment, and education. These are not merely obstacles but are the crucibles where innovation and technological maturity are forged.

As we move forward, let us carry these lessons of clarity and grounded expectations. This foundation prepares us to explore the limitless possibilities that await when vision aligns with scientific progress. In the next chapter, we will venture into the transformative potential that quantum technologies promise. Here, we will delve into the societal implications, future applications, and ethical considerations of living in a quantum-enhanced world. Let us continue this journey with an open mind, ready to embrace both the envisioned dreams and the pragmatic reality of the quantum frontier.

CONCLUSION:
"QUANTUM FRONTIER"

As we reach the end of our journey through the "Quantum Frontier," it is time to distill the profound insights, cutting-edge concepts, and transformative strategies that have been explored within these pages. By unraveling the intricate weave of quantum mechanics, we have ventured from its theoretical foundations to its burgeoning applications poised to redefine industries and societies alike.

At the heart of our exploration lies the essence of quantum computing: a technology born from the subatomic mysteries of the universe, now poised to reinvent our relationship with information. From the qubit's dance of superposition to the tangled embrace of entanglement, you have navigated this complex terrain under the guidance of pioneering scientists and visionaries who have charted this brave new world. Chapter by chapter, you've witnessed how quantum computing is set to surpass the capabilities of classical computing, offering unprecedented solutions in sectors such as cryptography, drug discovery, artificial intelligence, and beyond.

The insights gleaned throughout this narrative underscore a fundamental truth: quantum technology is not just a future aspiration—it is a present reality with profound implications for every sector it touches. By harnessing the capabilities outlined in this book, readers are equipped to enhance personal and professional trajectories. The emergence of quantum computing offers not only a new realm of technological possibility but also a transformational vision of humanity's potential.

Now is the time to act. As quantum technology advances from laboratory to industry, every reader holds the potential to be a catalyst in this revolution. Whether you are an innovator, educator, advisor, or enthusiast, the invitation to be a trailblazer in the quantum age is yours to accept. Embrace this period of rapid paradigm shifts by participating in discourse, education, and collaborative endeavors within this transformative field.

In closing, recall the speculative vistas we have sketched together, imagining a world where quantum technology addresses the existential challenges of our time and fosters a future replete with sustainable and equitable progress. This vision of tomorrow is grounded not just in technological possibility but in human ingenuity and resilience. As you step away from these pages, remember that you are now part of this quantum lineage—a growing legion of thinkers and dreamers dedicated to forging a path toward a more enlightened, connected world.

It is with optimism and conviction that I remind you: the horizon of quantum technology is not a distant mirage but a beacon beckoning those with the courage and curiosity to explore. With purpose and passion, let us embrace this transformative epoch, understanding that the true quantum revolution is not just in technology—but within the limitless potential of human imagination.

ACKNOWLEDGMENTS

Writing "Quantum Frontier: Demystifying the Next Tech Revolution" has been an extraordinary journey, marked by moments of deep inquiry, relentless dedication, and the unwavering pursuit of clarity in the enigmatic realm of quantum technology. This book would not have been possible without the confluence of inspiration, guidance, and support from numerous individuals who have played pivotal roles in shaping my professional path and vision.

First and foremost, I wish to express my profound gratitude to the thought leaders in the field of technology and quantum physics whose groundbreaking work has laid the foundation for this book. Figures like Richard Feynman, whose visionary ideas on quantum computing first ignited a revolution in thinking, and John Preskill, who continues to illuminate the path with his insights into quantum information science, have been a constant source of inspiration. Their dedication to pushing the boundaries of what we understand has profoundly influenced my own journey and solidified my commitment to making these complex subjects accessible and engaging.

I am deeply thankful to my family and friends who have been my bedrock of support throughout this endeavor. To my loving spouse and children, your patience and encouragement fueled my perseverance during long nights of writing and research. Your belief in my work has been my greatest motivator.

My heartfelt thanks also go to my editor and publisher, whose keen insights and unwavering support helped refine and elevate this book to its fullest potential. To the brilliant minds and collaborators who shared countless discussions and debates, your enthusiasm and expertise have enriched this work immeasurably.

Lastly, I encourage you, dear reader, to cherish and recognize the individuals and experiences that propel you toward your goals. Success is rarely a solitary pursuit; it is a tapestry woven from perseverance, collaboration, and the wisdom of those who came before us. May this book serve as a reminder of the vibrant power of shared knowledge and the boundless possibilities that await when we dare to venture into the quantum frontier together.

Author Biography

Richard Drayton stands at the forefront of quantum computing literature, his narrative artistry seamlessly weaving science and imagination in ways accessible to both novice and expert alike. Raised in the vibrant, innovation-driven atmosphere of San Francisco, Richard's journey into the world of technology began in his grandfather's eclectic workshop. The amalgam of gadgets and scientific wonders within ignited a lifelong passion for exploring the frontiers of physics and digital technology. It was in this environment that Richard's appreciation for the intricacies of the quantum world began to take shape.

Richard's professional trajectory is marked by deep-seated expertise and visionary thought leadership in the field. Before dedicating himself to writing full-time, he gained invaluable insights and experience as a senior technology consultant. This role allowed him to delve into the practical implications of quantum computing, working alongside some of the most innovative minds, and gaining firsthand exposure to the transformative potential of this burgeoning technology. His transition from consulting to authorship involves a merging of scientific discipline and speculative foresight, enabling him to demystify complex concepts while projecting future advancements that tantalize the imagination.

His oeuvre, including "Quantum Frontier: Demystifying the Next Tech Revolution," showcases his ability to transform the academic rigor of quantum theory into narratives underscored by real-world relevance and potential. Drawing from a career at the juncture of technological innovation and research, Richard crafts stories that not only inform but inspire. By bridging the traditional foundations of science with pioneering innovation, he has established himself as a trustworthy and authoritative figure, capable of guiding readers through the maze of tomorrow's technological revolutions. Through his works, Richard Drayton invites us to not only understand the quantum realm but to embark on a journey of curiosity and wonder, making complex ideas accessible and compelling to a global audience eager to engage with the next tech revolution.

Sources of Content

The foundational ideas and strategies within "Quantum Frontier: Demystifying the Next Tech Revolution" are drawn from a confluence of practical experience, technical principles, and evolving industry trends. Richard Drayton leverages his profound professional insights and hands-on background in technology consultation, ensuring that the material presented is both relevant and applicable to contemporary and future technological landscapes. These insights are augmented through comprehensive analyses of prevailing business models and sector-specific strategies, providing a well-rounded understanding of quantum computing's anticipated impact across multiple domains.

Moreover, the book's narrative is enriched with generative

analysis utilizing advanced AI tools, including ChatGPT, which synthesizes information from a wealth of relevant sources, examples, and case studies. This integration not only enhances the depth of content but also ensures the inclusion of diverse perspectives and the latest advancements in quantum technology. By blending his vast experience with cutting-edge editorial tools, Richard crafts a narrative that is at once powerful, practical, and prescient, offering readers valuable insights into the potential future of quantum computing.

Through this multifaceted approach, "Quantum Frontier" emerges as a vital resource for understanding quantum technology's trajectory and its transformative potential. The book's methodology exemplifies the intersection of expert knowledge and innovative editorial practices, creating an engaging and educational narrative that empowers readers to grasp and engage with a field poised to redefine our technological and societal horizons.